Communicating
Your Passion

A Personal and Practical Call to Rekindle the
Passion in Your Preaching

D. S. Briggs

*****Fourth Printing*****
ISBN 979-8-218-87023-2
Voice of Rehoboth Publishing
Woodson Terrace, MO. 63134
(314) 764 - 5168
dsbdr@hotmail.com

Dedication

To my mother who constantly challenged me to excel in all situations and would never let me be satisfied where I was.

To my father whom I do not know,
And yet... I love.

Table of Contents

Foreword

I have had the cherished privilege of knowing Dr. David Shawn Briggs for more than ten years. I have also been privileged to share in his ministry. I can't remember when I knew beyond a shadow of a doubt that God had placed in him a certain savoir-faire of exegetical analysis and expository ability.

Hearing him, not only in his preaching, but merely in his conversation, with exactness, speak as one having authority, with profound simplicity, having clarity of the context, the anointed genius of the overall presentation, I became convinced that he was and is "something special" in the Kingdom of God.

As I write this foreword, I must admit that I have a sense of pride that Dr. Briggs has finally been persuaded by those of us who have been prevailing upon him to put to print the exegetical genius that has emerged from his experience as a man, and as a minister of the Gospel of Jesus Christ. Anyone who reads this book and leaves with a feeling that its contents are insignificant to their ministry, has no idea how much they really need what is contained in its pages.

Communicating Your Passion reveals a very personal and insightfully practical approach to help the practitioners of preaching to rekindle their passion for and their confidence in both preparing to and the presenting of the Gospel message. I firmly believe that anyone who is authentically called (commanded) by God to preach the Gospel, if they grasp the truth found in this book, regardless of their formal theological training, or lack thereof, will be able to present messages that will give their listeners the ability to truly hear the Gospel. It will help the practitioner to develop a healthy relationship with God and in the preaching sense to renew a right spirit within (them).

I am certain the library of every preacher will be enhanced by the addition of this publication. For those persons who must acknowledge a call, but have yet to accept it, this book is a must.

I am thankful for the opportunity to be a part of such a wonderful effort as this and I look forward to the future as I hope Dr. Briggs will share himself in print again. To God be the Glory for the things He has done and is doing in Dr. David Shawn Briggs.

Jeffrey L. Reaves, Sr.
Chester, Virginia
January 2000

Acknowledgements

I am deeply indebted to all those that labored in love with me to complete this project. Those that have fasted and prayed for me, read and reviewed this manuscript at its various stages, those who offered their encouragement and constructive criticism, those who aided in the typing and the final of the manuscript. I bless the Lord for all of you and pray His Divine blessings are richly heaped upon you for what you have done.

First all glory goes to God for entrusting these gifts of His grace to me, the least of the brethren. To He who redeemed me by His blood and saved me by His grace. For the health, strength, ability and opportunity that He has given me to be obedient to Him. I owe my all to you.

Second, to my three pastors and their spouses who have blessed me and encouraged me in the things of God:

Rev. James L. Barnes, who has been more than a father in the ministry to me, but a friend as well. Thank you for instilling within me a passion for preaching that burns brightly till this day…a commitment to practice what I preach…an eye to see the entirety of the text and not be satisfied with a mere skimming over the surface…to see the people behind the problems they present…and the boldness to stand on the courage of

3

my convictions.

Rev. J. L. Reaves, Sr. ....my "brother" pastor who ministered to me at the lowest and darkest points of the ministry. You are my leaning tree with whom I can just let it be. Thank you for your compassion and friendship... your ability to see the unusual points and principles in familiar texts... an excellent example in effective communication in telling the story... one who can "say it well" and with authority... one that has been elevated high but yet still takes the time to help those who are aspiring one day to climb.

Rev. Dr. Frank S. Harrison.....my "professor" pastor who has diligently taught me both ethics and example. You have patiently put up with me as I matured in the ministry from a neophyte trying to find my way to a servant showing others the way. Thank you for being my "Gamaliel".... Encouraging me to get learning to go along with the burning and allowing me to just sit at your feet.

To all those ministers of the gospel that read and reviewed this manuscript in parts and the whole. I thank the Lord for your candor and willingness to assist in this project. Special thanks to Dr. C. L. Easley. Jr. of York, Pa., Rev. Marc Napoleon of New Orleans, La., Rev. K. Ed. Copeland III of Kankakee, Il., Rev. Darren Phelps of Miami, Fl., Rev. Horace B. Parham, Jr. of Petersburg, Va., Rev. Boyd A. Bullock, Sr. of Clifton Forge, Va., Dr. Alfred Thompson of Richmond, Va., Rev. Veronica Leach and Minister Agnes Seaborne of Emporia, Va., and Rev. Joseph Simmons of Petersburg, Va.

To all the pastors around the country that had faith to allow me to preach in their pulpits sometimes sight unseen and unheard. And to those who had the courage to ask me to come back.

I wish to thank **Rev. Dr. G. V. Guns**, President of the Virginia Baptist State Convention and **Rev. Steve Bland**, President of the Young Pastors and Ministers Department of the National Baptist Convention, USA, Inc. for their constant admonition at many conventions and conferences to all who would hear to... "write down what the Lord has blessed you with.....Don't take it to the grave with you." Their constant challenges for all of the ministers of the gospel to put in print what they are practicing and producing in their local parishes regardless to where they are pastoring have strengthened me for this work.

Thank you to Ms. Leah Shepperson, my secretary who has typed, retyped this manuscript, sent numerous e-mails requests for information, and sacrificed herself to bring this together. All of this while going to school full time and working full time. May God ever bless you for your sacrifice. We now await your album to drop!

Thank you to the Mount Calvary Baptist Church where I served Senior Minister during the writing of this book. Thank you for your prayers and patience with me and for allowing me to serve you. I am humbled how the Lord brought us together and honored

He kept us together for five years. To God be the Glory for the great things he has done through you. I pray that it shall continue to be so.

To the Mount Zoar Baptist Church of Durham, North Carolina where I served as Pastor for the past three years. We thank the Lord for His Divine appointment of bringing us together as Pastor and people to discover as long as we have the favor and grace of God, nothing is impossible.

Finally, to the Rehoboth Covenant Bible Fellowship, of Raleigh-Durham, North Carolina that which the Lord has birthed in us through trials by fire and a flood of tears. Praise God for you and the awesome work that God has clearly laid on our hearts in and our hands. Let us focus in faith, follow and fulfill all that the Lord has in store for us For **now** the Lord has made room for us and we shall be fruitful in this land!

Section I

Purpose

"For there is a time there for every purpose and for every work"
Ecclesiastes 3:17 c

The question penetrated a tender part of my soul, sharply driven to a place that only the Lord, my Pastor, my wife and I knew so well. The fears of inadequacy were raised and the frustrations of insecurity resurrected by this teasing and taunting question that was posed to me by another preacher. What qualifies me to write this book, let alone any book? I am not an English or a Literature major. I did not go to school to be a journalist or a writer. I certainly do not have the notoriety or name recognition necessary to be successful. I do not pastor a large or a well-known church, have a mega or major ministry, or have the reputation as an outstanding up and coming preacher. I am not known outside the local area that I presently serve. I am not on the revival circuit, and I did not graduate from the right schools. So, what qualifies me of all people to propose to write a book on such a daunting premise as preaching? Even if I was (and that was a stretch I was told) to complete the manuscript who would publish it and who would buy it.

I had nothing...no platform...no public acclaim...no money...no connections...nothing at all to ensure that any book that I would write could and would sell or even be in demand. Certainly not by any well established and recognized pastors. Why even waste my time and energy on a project that was so sure to fail?

Like Moses I found myself again wrestling with all the problems of responding to a Divine Challenge. More than once the haunting laments of "Who am I;

I'm not worthy; They will not believe me; Send someone else!" screamed to drop my pen and paper and to abandon the computer keyboard to write something that I am far more comfortable with, namely sermons. The pain of past battles rushed to my mind, driven recklessly by the demons of hell as I recalled all the times from my youth up I was told what I would never be, what I would never accomplish, what I could never achieve. No matter how good I was at whatever I did; there was always someone close to me that was better than me and some people seemed to take great pleasure in pointing this out to me as often as they could.

That spirit of negativity that had frustrated me in my purpose all my life was raised again from the dead to wage a war against the completion of this book. These highlighted issues from within and without could easily impede any meaningful progress in this project if I allowed them to become the focus of my life. I would then be walking in defeat and not in victory, dissuaded from the directions that the Lord had given me. Frustrations would then eventually pave the road to an expected failure. What if my interrogator was right? Why not just keep it to myself and thereby keep the peace?

Thankfully, the Holy Spirit brought back to my remembrance a quote that I had read a long time ago from Tertullian. This theologian stated in a most provocative way, "He who lives only to benefit himself, confers on the world a benefit when he dies."

Knowing that I now strive to live my life to be a

blessing to others, I had to make a determined effort to reject the negative spirit that had been just sent my way, unawares by this preacher. Perhaps he had good intentions and meant no real harm. But I had to reject the message that he brought. Instead, I focused on another set of questions, put forward to me by another minister not too long ago. His questions were a synopsis of many discussions that I have had with many other ministers. However, this was to be a special occasion. It was through this encounter that the Lord spoke to me and gave me the release to write this manuscript.

This release occurred while I attended the 1999 Hampton Minister's Conference. It did not come through the preachers and pastors that served as lecturers, presenters or proclaimers of the gospel. It did not occur during the high time of Worship and Praise. It did not even occur in one of those fragments of fraudulent fellowship that takes place in the numerous vending areas of the conference.

It was while I was visiting the home of another minister who was unable to attend the conference. During that visit he began to share his pain and burden of how he wished he could attend certain functions but could not because of insufficient finances and he was wondering when his opportunity would come. He was frustrated with ministers allegedly saying they would give him an opportunity to preach for them or they would recommend him to preach at vacant churches in the area and yet the phone never rang. He wondered what he was doing wrong and what he could do to improve his preaching. Here in the privacy of his own home, away from the "pomp and circumstance" of the ministry, he felt free to be honest and open about his pain. Listening to him describe his personal experience, reminded me of some of my own experiences. Perhaps some of yours as well.

The anguish of the people and preachers criticizing you because you were not ordained into the gospel ministry. Until you were called to pastor a church, ordination was completely out of the question. This prevented frustrated ministers who had not been called to a church yet from running out and starting up their own little "me and my family" church because they were too impatient one minister told me. How often were the words of Paul invoked by the preachers and pastors that had already attained to those of us who were just waiting for a chance "Or ministry, let us wait on our ministering." (Romans 12:7) Another said that the license was all you needed to do whatever ministry you had to do until (and if) you were eventually given the opportunity to pastor. Still another stated that it was purely a "Virginian quirk" on being ordained quickly. For in other states going ten to fifteen years before ordination was normal while in Virginia if you have not been ordained in two years both churches and clergy, pulpit and pew look askance and wonder openly "What is wrong with them?"

Yet some of those same churches would end up throwing your resume in the corner because they were specifically looking for someone that was already ordained. They wanted someone "already qualified" as one church told me. You may have been good enough to preach for them for three or four months in a row, but they let you know up front that they were not seriously considering you if you were not already ordained. However you could not be ordained until a church called you. It made you feel like an incomplete person and there was nothing that you could do to remedy the situation.

I remember vividly one deacon at a church in Buckingham County, Virginia cornered me one Sunday and literally grilled me like a jailhouse lawyer as to why I was not ordained. He wanted know if I had been arrested, divorced, or anything else that should in his opinion disqualify me from being ordained. In other words, what is wrong with me that I am not ordained? Being young in the ministry - about two years at that time - and having been taught to always respect my elders whether right or wrong, I patiently heard him out.

Finally, I replied to him that ultimately it was strictly my Pastor's decision as to when I was to be ordained with the church's consent and that would only occur if I were called to pastor a church. All I was doing was being obedient and in submission to the authority that the Lord had placed me under. But his parting shot still rings in my ear. "Preacher, **until you are ordained you will never be a full minister**; you won't be able to function by yourself and these churches aren't going to call you if you still got those apron strings tied around you." The funniest thing is that the church he was a member of already had a pastor. I was preaching for another church in the area, which did eventually vote and extend the call for me to be their pastor. Even though I was not ordained.

So many ministers are seeking to establish their own ministries and reputation amongst the ecclesiastical elite, offering every type of conceivable inducement, both godly and ungodly, to be a part of their ministerial staff. They wanted to have some "Holy Ghost" bookends or several "Sons of Thunder" to call their own. "Just leave where you are and join my church or denomination" they say and instant ordination, staff positions – which are a great resume builder by the way, some type of salary, office space and many other perks are yours. Even Pastors whose churches were not looking for or did not need that type of ministry offered these. All to shape another pastors ego and to build him up so that he would have more to brag about on his resume.

Pastors who perhaps in good faith that always asked for a card and told you and everybody else within earshot that you will be with him this year and…. "I want you to bring the word, young man" who never called. When you see them time after time they keep on reminding you that "I haven't forgotten you, I'll call you this week and set up a date." But the telephone never rings. However, they never seem to be a loss of reminding you that they somehow encouraged you when and if you finally do become a pastor, because they want to come preach your installation message or to preach your revivals for you. The sad thing is that many of them have an oppressive and negative attitude towards you if you do not invite them to preach for you. They act like you think that you are too good for them "now that you've arrived" when in reality you are glad that the door has been opened to give you a chance to be a pastor of God's people.

Have you been there?

As I began to minister to him from the Word of God and from my limited experience the Lord spoke to me and told me that here was somebody that was willing to hear what I had to say and that there were many, many others just like him. It did not matter to him what size the church I pastor was, how much money I made, what positions I held, what school I went to, or when my next revival meeting was. If I would just be obedient to the Lord, then there would be somebody willing to take the time to read and listen to what God has given me and somebody would be helped. The true question was I willing to make the sacrifice?

After prayer and leaving that home to return to the conference the Lord showed me how I had neglected to do in the past what he had told me again that night. The concept for this book along with many others had been birthed in my spirit eight years ago. Yet they never came to fruition because the twins of insecurity and inadequacy aborted them, never to see the light of day. This project has been delayed due to a paralysis of personal analysis. My own as to the content and what I thought others would criticize the book as beneath their personal level of expertise or because it was not written by the Pastor of a major "house" so what cold he possibly say to help me? I did not want to write this book strictly from a theological platform but rather from a personal one. I was so concerned over what other people said that I was not qualified to be and do and had the mentality that only successful people, who are successful by meeting or exceeding standards that are often set by others and not themselves, write books. Since I did not consider myself to be successful by the standards that my questioner now raised, then I had no need to write a book.

The Lord showed me the need to write this book from a different perspective. Not as one that has already attained or achieved fame, honor or recognition. **Simply as one preacher to another.** Friend to friend. Simple, honest words of encouragement and empowerment for those that suffer for the cause and cross of Christ. As a preacher, looking to be a better preacher seeking down to earth and honest help to aid me on my journey. One who understands the cries of many frustrated preachers because I too have been a frustrated preacher.

God has given me, by His grace a gift for writing. Too long latent, this gift has been with me from my youth and had been silenced for too long due to my heeding the negative voices in my life. Through this innocuous conversation with my fellow co laborer, God so graciously forgave me for sitting on the gift that He gave me and gave me another chance.

I write this book with the fervent prayer that we as ministers of the Gospel of Grace will rekindle the fire and fervor of our preaching. Preaching, in general, has become too dry eyed and too dry period. Performance has been elevated over proclamation; Show over sincerity; Style over substance; "whoop" over hope; Gossip over the Gospel. It has become cold, practiced and passionless!

Where are the burning fires of repentance and revival that burn the chaff and dross out of our lives? They cannot start to burn in our churches unless the pastors that God has ordained bring the light! If there is no praise, no prayers and no passion from the pews then perhaps one ought to check out what is going on in the pulpit.

Where are those who will not only declare like Queen Esther *"If I perish, I perish."* but live it as well? (Esther 4:16 e) Where are the modern day Paul's who declare *"For me to live is Christ and to die is gain."* (Philippians 1:21) And again *"So as much as in me is, I am ready to preach the gospel to you that are at Rome also. For I am not ashamed of the gospel of Christ: for it is the power of God unto salvation for everyone that believeth"* (Romans 1:15-16) Where are the powerful preachers like Peter who understand *"If any man speak, let him speak as the oracles of God; if any man minister, let him do it as of the ability which God giveth: that God may be glorified through Jesus Christ, to whom be praise and dominion forever and ever. Amen."*

Where is the passion? Where is the burden? Where are the intercessors? Where is the preaching with power that is able to change lives? Where are the weeping prophets?

"Let the priests, the ministers of the Lord weep between the porch and the altar, and let them say, Spare thy people O Lord..." (Joel 2:17)

Preaching must once again reclaim the prominence and pre eminence in the life of the local congregation. But it must start with the heart of the preacher. If the preacher has no passion for the God that they are preaching about then how can they reasonably expect that the people will be excited about God? Rev. J. L. Reaves, Sr., the pastor of the Good Shepherd Baptist Church in Petersburg Virginia and my pastor puts it quite bluntly when he says *"Until you generate a passion for the things of God, God will never give you a position."*

God won't give it to you. Man might, but not God. I have discovered through the controversy of confirmed circumstances that whatever man gives you they can take away. Whenever man puts you up, he can pull you down, but when God raises you up, there is no man or woman, or devil alive and kicking that can stop God from being God and doing what he is doing in your life.

We as ministers have focused on so many other Programs, building projects, surviving one more week or just holding on until someone else calls us to another pastorate, civic responsibilities and dare I say it - money making schemes and dreams that the priority of preaching has often been placed last on our things to do list. We are saved neither by fundraisers, glad handing, local elections, choir competitions nor by building beautification; but we are saved by and through the preaching of the gospel of Jesus Christ. The Apostle Paul says it best....

"... it pleased God by the foolishness of preaching to save them that believe...." (I Corinthians1:21)

Even as we seek to develop ministries to minister to the various needs of the people we serve, we dare not think so lightly of the Ministry of the Word of God! We ought to give it a proper place in our affections and devotion. Preaching, and the preparation for preaching in particular should not be a discipline of left over time. Eternity hangs in the balance! Eternal Life or Eternal Damnation! Preach with a heart for the unsaved! Everybody in your community or your church is still not saved. There are many people that live right around the corner from your church that have passed through the revolving door of church membership. They may be a "member of _____ Church," but they have not attended any church in many years. Throw out the lifeline! Preach the blessings and the woes of the Book! Preach Heaven open and hell revealed! Preach the rumbling of Sinai and the wooing of Calvary! Preach! So that a downtrodden people shall rejoice with the victorious claim of the Psalmist…

"Lift up your heads, O ye gates; and be ye lift up, ye ever-
lasting doors and the King of Glory shall come in.

Who is this King of Glory? The Lord strong and mighty,
The Lord mighty in battle. Lift up your heads O ye gates;
even lift them up ye everlasting doors; and the King of
Glory shall come in. Who is this King of glory???   The Lord
of Hosts… He is the King of glory!!!"   [Psalm 24:7-10]

That we will effectively communicate our passion with Holy zeal is the purpose of this book. That we will work together as co laborers in the Kingdom regardless of school affiliation or pastoral location is our plea. That even one minister is blessed by reading this book and willing to press on is our prayer.

1

The Call to be in His Presence

*"All that the Father giveth me shall come to me; and him
that cometh to me I will in no wise cast out."*
St John 6:37

I am not called to preach.

To some that have just picked up this book on
preaching written by a preacher and a pastor, this may
seem to be a blasphemous statement. After all the receiving of "the call" is a spiritual mandate that must be
if we dare to proclaim ourselves to be a preacher of the
Lord. There is no calling on earth so noble and righteous as the call to preach. It is greater than the Presi-
dency, more powerful than Congress, adjudicates more
cases than the Supreme Court and has the ability to ex-
ert more financial control in the lives of the people of
God than the Federal Reserve.

Lest I be accused of being a heretic, having denied
the faith and worse than an infidel, let me assure you

that I know beyond a shadow of a doubt that I have been called. It is settled, safe, and secure in my spirit. I would stake my life on it and die victoriously for my belief in it. I have been called. I just have not been called to preach.

Let us read St. Mark 3: 13-15

*"And He goeth up into a mountain, and calleth **unto Him** whom He would: and they came unto Him.*

And He ordained twelve, that they should be with Him, and that He might send them forth to preach,

And to have power to heal sicknesses, and to cast out devils."

Upon reading this text to prepare to teach a workshop for Associate Ministers for my State Convention, the Lord revealed something to me so profound that it was perplexing.

> I did not call you to preach.
> I called you to come into my presence.
> I commanded you to pursue after me.
> I commissioned you to preach.

What I believe that the Lord has called us to do as evidenced in this text is to come unto Him. A compatriot of mine would say to "make movement from our mess to ministry." The call of Jesus Christ is to leave from where we are, wherever we are, to ascend to where He is. When we leave where we were, what we have become and what we have become comfortable with to seek new possibilities for life on the Mountain with the Lord. Notice what happens when the apostles followed the Lord's command. When questioned by Annas the high priest, Caiaphas, John, Alexander while setting in the midst of the rulers and elders, the boldness of Peter and John. The Bible declares:

"Now when they saw the boldness of Peter and John, and perceived that they were unlearned and ignorant men, they marveled: and they took knowledge of them, that they had been with Jesus."
(Acts 4:13)

They did not notice the cut of their clothes, the school from which they matriculated or graduated or the size or budget of the church that they were serving. They did not notice anything that we might look for today in a preacher of the gospel. According to the text, their perception was that both Peter and John were not only unlearned but ignorant. Yet they still marveled. Why? They noticed that they had been with Jesus.

Does the world take notice that we have been with the Lord? What about the communities that we serve or the churches we pastor? What about our family? Or are we so busy highlighting temporal achievements that will soon lose their luster that Jesus becomes a mere byword in our conversation?

They can tell what school we went to by the way we preach but can they tell that we have been with Jesus?

They can tell our devotion to cultivating our theological education based on the certificates, diplomas, or degrees hanging on the study walls, but can they tell we have been with Jesus?

They can tell what "camp of preachers" (or should I say clique?) we are in based on the clothes we wear and who we let come and preach for us but can they tell that we have been with Jesus?

Our call and our mandate is to follow Jesus and dwell in His Holy presence. Rev. Dr. G. V. Guns, Senior Pastor at the Second Calvary Baptist Church in Norfolk, Virginia and the President of the Virginia Baptist State Convention writes in *"The Empowered Ministry: Achieving Effectiveness in Ministry"* "The call to Christian ministry is first and foremost the call to follow Jesus. No man or woman should even think of going into ministry who does not first acknowledge that we are called to follow Jesus Christ. Jesus never called men to follow noble ideas, great causes, nor ambitious people, rather it was a clear call to follow him.' (1)

It is after this call that I discover the paradigm for preaching with passion. It serves not only as the platform for this writing, but as the foundation for the ministry that the Lord as so graciously allowed me to have and my personal life as well. To encapsulate it briefly....

Presence develops Passion
Passion discovers Purpose
Purpose determines Position
Position demands Power

I know that will preach!

1. When you are in the **presence** of the Lord you will develop a **passion** for the things of God.

2. When your **passion** for the things of God is developed, it leads you to discovering your **purpose** in the Kingdom of God.

3. Once you discover your **purpose** (and it only happens when you are in His presence) the Lord will commission you to **pursue** what He has revealed to you.

4. It is a possibility that He may send you forth to many divergent ministries while not necessarily sending you forth to preach. **This is the pivot of the text for me.** It is observing and being obedient to what we **must** do (come unto Him) versus what we **might** do.
   (to preach)

5. Christ commissions us to fulfill His purpose and places us in **position** to accomplish His will.

6. Every **position** that the Lord gives you demands His **power** in order to complete His plan.

What I have discovered is that many preachers, just like many church leaders reverse the above order. They desire a **position** (pastor) so that they may feel like that they are fulfilling some positive **purpose** for the Lord. (Insecurity, low self esteem) This then drives them to be passionate about their purpose because their self-worth is rooted in their position. ("If I become Chairman, Trustee, Pastor, President, etc., then I will really do some work for the Lord and my church!") Finally this new found **passion** will make (or force) them to spend time in the **presence** of God. No wonder it is so difficult to change leaders at many churches. Their position validates who they "think" they are in God. Take that away from them and you have a fight on your hands. It is all that some people have.

Have you ever been there?

Would you be willing to just be in His presence? No commission, no job, no Christian organizations to be the chairperson of, no other responsibility or duty but to just be in the presence of Almighty God. Just to know that you are in His will and have followed in His way. The **call** is to come from where you are, take the journey and be in the presence of the Lord. The **command** is to be in God's presence. The **charge** is that the Lord may send us forth from His presence after we have followed and observed Him. The **commission** is that we might be sent forth to preach the gospel of Jesus Christ.

That is what the Lord has called me to do. Not to be the city-wide revivalist three years in a row. Not to have a mega ministry or to pastor the largest church in town. Not to be President or Moderator or Chairperson of any Christian Faith Organization. Not to be on City Council or the Board of Supervisors. My faithfulness and obedience to the command of Christ may indeed open up those doors for me, but these things are not my chief joy, concern, or obsession.

Just to be in His presence.

"Surely the righteous shall give thanks unto thy name: the upright shall dwell in thy presence."
(Psalm 140:13)

"... we stand before this house, and in thy presence (for thy name is in this house,) and cry unto thee in our affliction, then thou will hear and help."
(II Chronicles 20:9)

William C. Martin in his book *"To Fulfill This Ministry"* writes *"...* if the Christian religion is to demand and secure men's deepest loyalties it must speak again with an authority that is born of a first hand contact with God." (2)

When the word authority is used in connection with God or the things of God as revealed in the Scriptures, it means the absolute power and freedom to do whatever the Lord chooses. The ability to speak with such authority is not developed in seminary or Bible College. You might be able to, upon graduation, speak **as** an authority but not necessarily **with** authority. The teachers and professors will convey information to you and fill you with factual knowledge, historical perspectives, homiletic preciseness, and hermeneutic possibilities. You will and should be able to speak a coherent well-organized presentation, but not with the authority needed in truly effective preaching. To preach or to speak with an anointing on your life and authority to break the shackles of sin, loose the handcuffs of hurt and to set the captives free is only birthed out of the necessary discipline of being in the presence of God. It is the anointing of the Lord that empowers the minister of the Gospel to stand and declare both with authority and as an authority "Thus says the Lord!" The anointing of God is not passed on to you in seminary, nor by family ties; it only comes from prostrating oneself continually in the presence of the Lord, and submitting oneself to His Lordship in their life.

In no way am I belittling the above mentioned accomplishments or am I jealous over those in those capacities. I hold many of those positions even now at the time of this writing. The burden on my heart is that we as ministers seek so much for what the world and even our pastoral peers define as success that we lose sight of what is really important. Our priorities get out of order. The decision of who will retain "our services" as the next Pastor of _____ Church, much like a free agent in professional sports is more often than not sold out to the highest bidder. Preaching and serving as a Pastor becomes a means to an end. Just another way for some to pay their bills and not the result of a passion that has been developed in the presence of the Lord.

We have lost our passion. Preaching sermons become something we do and not something we are. Jerry Vines says "The preacher not only delivers his sermon; he also delivers himself." (3) The process of preparing sermons too often becomes as mechanical as developing a fill in the blank order form. Once the form is filled out, the sermon is done. The eternal impart of our proclamation is often diminished and invariably summed up by the following questions:

- Did we have church?
- Did the people worship and praise as we think they should have?
- Did they shout?
- How many people joined?
- How much money did we take in?
- Did I really preach well today?"

The blessed assurance of the Lord is that we can reclaim our passion. The fires of repentance, revival, and renewal can once again be set ablaze in our ministries. The power of the Lord can fall fresh and infuse your local congregation. The people of God who come tired, hungry and thirsty can look forward to fresh manna whenever you stand and not a "heat, eat and take a seat" micro-waved meal. How do you ask?

Learn to be in His presence. In His presence is the fullness of Joy. (Psalm 16:11) Take the time to commune with the Lord every day. Do not disregard the importance of having a daily devotional time. Do not wait for Saturday night to get down on your knees, begging for a "word from the Lord." When you spend time in

His presence. You will always have a word. It may not fit into your preferred format of preaching but you will always have a word in season for those that are weary. (Isaiah 50:4)

Rekindle your desire to worship God. The Lord makes us as first and foremost creatures of worship. It is defined in the Westminster Catechism as the first duty of man. There is in the spirit of every man and woman the need and desire to worship. In their book, *"Power in the Pulpit"* Jerry Vines and Jim Shaddix write:

"The preacher must know intimately the Author of the message he proclaims, if his ministry is to be built on a strong foundation... If the preacher falls in love with the Lord, he will love His Word. Such love of the Lord and the Bible will be conveyed enthusiastically to listeners in the preaching event. But just as the scientist may lose God in his test tube so the preacher may lose God in his study. He may become so involved in the mechanics of sermon preparation that he loses his awareness of the presence of God in his personal life. Consequently, the preacher must develop and nurture a vibrant practice of personal worship." (4)

We must worship. We will worship. We will worship something or somebody even if it is not God. Your worship starts at home, moves through the church and finds its fulfillment as you faithfully handle whatever the Lord has commissioned you to do. Those who do not worship in private do not worship in public. Eugene Peterson in his book entitled, *"Reversed Thunder"* warns us of the pitfalls if we fail to worship God and to keep worship at the center of our life:

"Failure to worship consigns us to a life of spasms and jerks, at the mercy of every advertisement, every seduction, every siren. Without worship we live manipulated and manipulating lives. We move either in frightened panic or deluded lethargy as we are in turn alarmed by specters and soothed by placebos. If there is no center, there is no circumference. People who do not worship are swept into a vast restlessness epidemic in the world with no steady direction and no sustaining purpose." (5)

So many of us preachers and pastors focus so much on the problems of our pastorates, making a living, being respected by other ministers, and quite often get so busy fulfilling our community obligations through various organizations that we fail to worship the Lord. How many of those community obligations, organizations, committees, or elected offices that take up so much of your time did God tell you to fulfill and no one else? We discover that in the Book of Acts, Chapter Six, the appointment and authorization of designated disciples for servant leadership was not only to answer the administrative/stewardship needs of a growing church, or to quell the smoldering fires of dissension that threatened the unity of the Early Church. It was to free the mind and ministry of the apostles for their passion. The apostles were to be in continual prayer and the ministry of the Word.

Learn to delegate tasks and delete some of your titles. Start a community outreach ministry that seeks to train your members to be more actively involved in the affairs of the community through the same organizations that are taking up so much of your time. Begin now to empower your members to take on these roles as you impart your spirit and vision into them, but preacher whatever you do, do not fail to worship.

It is amazing that many preachers of the gospel do not worship the Lord. They worship the church, their "package," their ability, their association, convention, and sad to say, some even worship themselves. Some preach and some perform. Some desire to be seen and others to be heard. But so many ministers do not worship. I did not say that they do not go to church. I did not say that they do not sing songs, pray prayers, or preach. I said that they do not worship God.

How can we lead in worship if we do not worship ourselves? They approach the pulpit and worship as a casual observer instead of an intentional participator. They see everything leading up to the sermon as a mere warm-up for what is really important, namely, what they have to say. Arms folded in such a body language position as to suggest that they are bored with the proceedings. Legs crossed as if they are sitting for a family portrait or a fireside chat. Yet when preaching time comes they come alive and wonder why people will not worship while they preach. It almost appears that when we respond to the commission of Christ to go and preach that we forget all about worship.

Preaching, if it is biblical is a direct result of our being in God's presence and is centered in our worship of God. It does not exclude us from the biblical commands to worship the Lord. There is a direct and defined correlation between our preaching and our worship. Merrill F. Unger advances this argument for preachers to worship when he says "It takes a long while for many otherwise able expositors to discover this simple fact. Others never realize it. As a result intellectuality rather than spirituality characterize their ministry. The letter of Biblical truth is illuminated, but (it is) not properly combined with the Spirit and the power of the Word." (6)

How can we neglect the Biblical commands to worship the Lord?

II Kings 17:36... *"But the Lord that brought you up out of the land of Egypt with great power and a stretched out arm, Him shall you fear, and Him shall you worship, and to Him shall you do sacrifice."*

Psalm 29:2... *"Give unto the Lord the glory due His name: worship the Lord in the beauty of holiness."*

Psalm 66:4... *"All the earth shall worship thee, and shall sing unto thee: they shall sing to thy name."*

Psalm 95:6... *"O come, let us worship and bow down: let us kneel before the Lord our maker."*

St. Matthew 4:10... *"Then saith Jesus unto him, 'Get thee hence, Satan: for it is written, Thou shall worship the Lord thy God, and only Him shalt thou serve.'"*

If we want to rekindle our passion for preaching, we must practice the presence of God in our lives. Our sense of worship should consume our preaching. In teaching my Bible Study class recently, a member asked a question about preaching in general. My response was that the very act of my preaching - the mere fact that I do preach the word of God is born not just out of my sense of the call of God but out of my desire to worship Him. My desire to worship God is strengthened when I dwell in His presence. It is another aspect of my personal worship that has been developed in my private time with the Lord. The things that I say, are given from the Lord, sharpened by research, and communicated in such a way that the people may sense the passion that I have about the God that I serve and to make up their minds to make or maintain a commitment with Jesus Christ in spite of the obstacles of life.

I am not called to preach. I am called to be in His presence.

2

The Command to Pursue

*"And Jesus, walking by the sea of Galilee, saw two breth-
ren, Simon called Peter, and Andrew his brother, casting a
net into the sea: for they were fishers. And He saith unto
them 'Follow me, and I will make you fishers of men.' And
they straightway left their nets, and followed Him."*
St. Matthew 4:18-20

As one learns to be in the presence of the Lord,
one is challenged with the prospect of following
the Lord. The command to follow the Lord calls for us
to put our priorities in order and to do first things first.
The call to follow often requires one to leave behind
anything (and if absolutely necessary, anyone) that will
keep you from fully following God. There is a definite
cost or sacrifice associated with following the Lord.
(see St. Luke 9:57-62)

Okechukwu Ogbonnaya in his book, *"In Step with
the Master"* details the perils of life following the

Master. He writes "If we listen to the voice of Jesus calling, we will see that Jesus means to transform our reality and create within us divine greatness. The power of this voice can create a new value within our being. But to do this, we must realize that we do not call ourselves. We cannot follow ourselves, for that is a vicious cycle that leads nowhere. But to follow we must listen to the voice of the divine Son of the living God. It is true that sometimes the voices that call us are not mainly that of Jesus or that of the devil or that of other human beings, but voices of our own conceit and deception. The only voice that we must listen and follow is the voice of the divine Son of God, even Jesus Christ. In His voice alone we find light and life. (7)

Dr. Miles Jerome Jones, Professor of Homiletics at Virginia Union University talks about the call to the follow the Lord is this light: "The call to follow Jesus is more than an invitation to come behind Him, as some of His disciples seemed to believe. Trailing Him as they did still did not allow them to perceive his purpose nor grasp the significance of His deeds.

Jesus nevertheless tolerates the shortcomings of those who would be His companions and does not hold their lack of understanding against them. It is a testimony to His compassion to allow the unperceiving followers of any age to still be with Him both as the journey is begun and the destination is reached." (8)

In this particular text, Peter and Andrew already had a living; they already had a lifestyle that they were accustomed to; they already had a life. They were fishermen. The fishing industry around the sea of Galilee was profitable enough for Peter and Andrew that they were actively engaged in the process of providing for their families. Yet here comes Jesus while they were in the process of taking care of their needs. He calls for them to stop fishing and start following. There were many voices crying out for man to follow them in that day. There were many false prophets and make believe messiahs. How did they know that they were following the right one? What if they were wrong?

Have you ever asked yourself what they would give up if they followed Jesus?

- They gave up their jobs.
- They gave up their careers.
- They gave up their business
- They gave up their ability to provide for their families
- They gave up fellowship in the Fraternal Order of Fishermen.
- They gave up a certain level of convenience and security.
- They gave up comfort and stability.
- They gave up their plans for their future.

Realistically speaking, if they were wrong, they would lose everything that they had. This would not be a journey based on facts, but rather on faith. An unknown pilgrimage following a yet unproven prophet. While Peter and Andrew may not of had all the riches and luxuries that the world had to offer, what little bit that they did have, they were now being asked to release and relinquish those things. Whatever minimal security and comfort they may of had, whatever prestige, whatever favor was to be cast aside just to follow Jesus.

The call to follow is the call to give up things that we have grown comfortable with. Things that can often adversely hinder our relationship with God. It often calls for a radical re-organization of ones life's goals and accomplishments. As Paul declares to the Philippian Church in chapter three and verse number 8…

"Yea, doubtless and I count all things but loss for the excellency for the knowledge of Jesus Christ my Lord: for whom I have suffered the loss of all things, and do count them but dung, that I may win Christ,"

To follow Jesus is a walk of sacrifice. It has never been a walk of luxury or ease. It calls for a level of sacrifice not often demanded in the secular world. To give up all comfort and pre-conceived plans as to what you will be, where you will go, were you will live, how much you will make and what will you achieve. Like Abraham, we find ourselves being obedient to the Lord and follow His direction, yet not knowing where we are going. Like Noah we prepare for that which others do not believe is possible and are ridiculed in the process. Like

Moses, we follow the Lord and end up returning to unfriendly surroundings and hostile situations simply because God told us to go. How well the hymnologist put it when she said

"Where He leads me I will Follow...
I'll go with Him
With Him
All the way." (9)

In the secular world, one often sacrifices time with their families to work extra long hours trying to get ahead, knowing that one day it will all be worth it. They attend countless meetings, sacrifice many years at the best University they can afford, burn the midnight oil and attend numerous workshops not for fellowship but to further their ambitions. They know that if they just invest that time now that more than likely one day they will be able to enjoy what they have earned. That raise and promotion will most certainly come. They will be able to, if necessary, make an upward transition to another company that will compensate them what they believe they are worth if they are not able to climb any higher in their present organization. They will be able to put money away for a rainy day or for retirement because they are receiving a living wage and a decent salary as opposed to a blessing wage or token salary. With prudent management, rarely will they have to rob Peter to pay Paul. They will be able to retire and live off of the fruits of their past labor.

However there is no such assurance for the man or

woman of God that has been selected to serve the Lord through the position of preacher or pastor. There is no guarantee that we will have all this world's riches, ease of life, trouble-free marriages, perfect and productive children, regardless of how much time, money, labor, or energy that we invest. There are no promises that the time and money we have invested in our seminary training will ever "pay off on this side of the Jordan." There are no promises that the churches we serve will remember our many years of labor as we advance in years. Many of our worst battles have centered around requesting the people of God to simply meet our needs so we can be free to minister without the inordinate stress of worrying how we are going to pay our bills on time, get out of debt, or stay out of debt. There is no promise that we will ever be elevated to a church that is larger (in ministry, members or money) than the one we currently serve no matter how faithful we have been or how long we have served. No promise that we will be respected or appreciated by those we serve or those who are our co-laborers in the gospel. We are not even given a timetable for the manifold more than blessing that the Lord promises to every one that has given up and forsaken houses, family, or lands for the Kingdom of God's sake. (see St. Luke 18:29-30) I understand that if I am faithful that He will remember my labor and service, but the repo man will not wait. The landlord wants his rent now. The bank is getting ready to foreclose on our home. If I don't pay this same phone bill that I ran up calling and checking on the members of the church that I pastor by 5:00 pm, the Telephone Company will disconnect my service. And yet we are still commanded to follow.

Our frustration rises and our faith falters as we begin to analyze the prospects of perpetual need crashing against the burdensome backdrop of projected wants. We have traded in our briefcases for a Bible...our careers for Christ...our professions for our preaching. And we wonder when it all will pay off. Like Peter we finally give voice to that which has vexed us

"Behold we have forsaken all and followed thee, what shall we have therefore?" (St. Matthew 19:27)

Haven't you ever wondered "What's in it for me?"

Yet in spite of the difficulties described, the down moments, we follow on. For it is only as we follow on that the Lord reveals His will for our lives. As we follow, we get stronger day by day. As we follow, our faith increases as we begin to see possibilities instead of problems. As we follow on, the picture, once fuzzy, begins to come into focus. As we follow on, everyday with Jesus gets sweeter than the day before.

"I have decided to follow Jesus
No turning back!
No turning back!' (10)

When we follow the Lord, we so often lift up the struggles. Yes, it is hard with Him but it is so much harder without Him! We forget that He has promised to:

Stay by our Side.
To give us:
Strength for the Struggle.
And He wants to:
Share in the Success

It does not start at the outset of the journey, but it takes some time. Just walk with the Master and worship Him. One day it will be all worth it.

3

The Commission to Preach

"For though I preach the gospel, I have nothing to glory of: for necessity is laid upon me; yea, woe is me if I preach not the gospel!"
1 Corinthians 9:16

The word commission is defined as "…authority to act for, in behalf of, or in place of another; an act of entrusting or giving authority…" (Webster's 7th New Collegiate Dictionary, pg. 166) To be commissioned to preach by the Almighty is to be entrusted to a task of both earthly and eternal importance. No one can put or place you in the pulpit to preach with power but the Lord. No praying saints, no determined pastor, no seminary dean, no one! To be sure many have been sent and many others just went. However if the Lord does not commission you to proclaim His Word, works and will from the pulpit as a preacher, then stay out of the pulpit!

Preaching is a task that no one that truly believes

in their heart that they are either qualified for or worthy of, yet we can not escape it. If you can stop preaching, then the Lord did not commission you to preach. He may have given you a message for a moment or a sermon for a season. K. Ed Copeland says that it could be either inspiration or indigestion. (11) But for the preacher that God has been anointed from their mother's womb like Jeremiah (Jeremiah 1:5) to be a preacher and a prophet, the words of Paul are correct "Woe is me if I preach not the gospel!" It truly is a charge that we absolutely have to keep. We cannot escape; we can run but we cannot hide. We are commissioned to preach after we have been called into His presence and gone through whatever He has dictated we must go through to prepare us to be commissioned into active duty.

An officer in the military receives their commission only after they have gone through the procedures as outlined by whatever particular branch of service that they are in. The procedures are not taught out in the field but at an appropriate training facility and in the presence of certified trainers. Regardless of their qualifications that have allowed them to apply to and subsequently be accepted in Officer Candidate School, they must go through the military process and procedure to learn about military life. No exemptions are allowed regardless of where one went to school. Once this initial training and education process is completed to the satisfaction of the military, one is then commissioned as an officer with appropriate rank. The newly commissioned officer is assigned to some particular duty station where they may fulfill the commission that they have received and put to use the training and education that they have received. At this point, they have initially learned just enough to be comfortable with their role and assignment. Further training once they arrive at duty stations will move them from being merely comfortable to being more competent in their duties. The focus shifts from theoretical instruction to practical application.

In like manner, the servant of the Lord must sign up to be in the Army of the Lord. God wants all to enlist yet twists no ones arm or forces any one to sign up for active duty. Once we have yielded to the clarion call of Christ we spend time learning as much as we can about Him. We study His word, memorize His commandments, and learn more about His Divine nature. Whenever He is satisfied and ready, He assigns us to a duty station and equips us to be able to function effectively at that duty station. Until He is ready, we are not ready! We may be willing but may not truly be able. He gifts us for the tasks that He has set before us. The shift is then made from theoretical instruction to practical application. Some of the things we have learned before in theory in His presence will now be put into practice out in the field.

Through the process of being in the presence of the Lord, worshipping Him and following Him wherever He leads us, I believe that the Lord commissions us for duty wherever He wills and whenever He wants. Our joy is that He considers worthy enough to be assigned any particular duty. He places us where He sees fit, when He sees fit and equips us to fulfill any task that He has assigned us to complete. We must realize that the Lord has not commissioned everyone to preach or to pastor. For so long we have de-emphasized and de-valued all the other areas and arenas that the Lord has ordained for effective ministry. The common thought has been, both in the pulpit and in the pews, that "if the Lord has called you to preach then He called you to pastor." Unfortunately, this unscriptural mantra and myopic methodology has destroyed more churches, ministries, ministers, and members by trying to force proverbial square pegs into round holes.

"And He gave some, apostles; and some, prophets; and some, evangelists; and some, pastors and teachers; For the perfecting of the saints, for the work of the ministry, for the edifying of the body of Christ; Till we all come in the unity of the faith, and of the knowledge of the Son of God, unto a perfect man, unto the measure of the stature of the fullness of Christ:" (Ephesians 4:11-16)

In the word of God He does not have preferential favorites based on the positions that He assigns. He does however give us the power necessary to fulfill that position. It is clear that all positions that are God ordained are linked to His eternal purpose and are to work together to glorify the Lord and to accomplish His will. The one that is commissioned to preach is no less in the sight of God than the one that is called to pastor.

They just have different functions and responsibilities. The evangelist is not greater than the teacher. And if I were to be extremely courageous and controversial I would venture out on a limb to say that the pastor is not greater than the deacon. They are both servants with different functions and responsibilities but one purpose. Our trouble lies in that we do not know what our role responsibilities are so we cross the line to take on someone else's roles.

The Lord has commissioned us to preach His word. Now it is time to prepare.

Notes for Section 1 Chapters 1 - 3

1. Rev. Dr. G. V. Guns, The Empowered Ministry, Copyright 1999
2. William C. Martin, "To Fulfill This Ministry" pg # 40 Copyright 1949 Abingdon Press: Nashville, TN.
3. Jerry Vines, A Guide to Effective Sermon Delivery, Copyright 1986 Moody Press Chicago, IL.
4. Jerry Vines and Jim Shaddix, Power in the Pulpit: How to Prepare and Deliver Expository Sermons pg # 59 Copyright 1999 Moody Press, Chicago, IL.
5. Eugene Peterson, "Reversed Thunder" pg # 59 Copyright 1988, Harper and Row, San Francisco, CA.
6. Merril F. Unger, Principles of Expository Preaching, Copyright 1955, Zondervan: Grand Rapids, MI. pg 61
A. Okechukwu Ogbonnaya, In Step with the Master pg 12 Copyright 1999 Urban Ministries, Inc., Chicago, IL.
7. Miles Jerome Jones "Come Follow Me" A Lenten Devotional Series pg # 1 Copyright 1988.
8. E.W. Blandy "Where He Leads Me" Selection # 168 New National Baptist Hymnal Copyright 1977 Triad Publications Thirty Fourth Printing July 1989

9. "I Have Decided to Follow Jesus" Selection # 164 New National Baptist Hymnal Attributed to an Indian Prince. Folk Melody from India.

10. Rev. K. Edward Copeland, J. D. "Riding in the Second Chariot: A Guide for Associate Ministers" pg # 1 Copyright 1999 PrayerCloset Publishing, Kankakee, Il.

Section II

Preparation

"Prepare thy work without, and make it fit for thyself in the field; and afterwards build thine house."
Proverbs 24:27

Pastor William T. Lee wearily stood up and stretched his stiff muscles. Glancing at the clock on his cluttered desk he sighed deeply. It was already well past 3:00 in the morning, yet all he had written down was a few unrelated ideas that bore no resemblance to a sermon anyone he knew would deliver.

"What is wrong with me tonight?" Lee exclaimed aloud to himself, more out of frustration than anything else. This was the longest dry spell he ever had. Grabbing the remote control to the television and changing the channels, Pastor Lee pondered the situation that he now faced. In just a few hours the worshippers at Bethel Church would gather to hear "a Word from the Lord." Here he was, the Lord's anointed, the Lord's messenger for the morning, without anything to say. The commentaries gave no new insight on the text he wanted to preach from. Calls made to his seminary friends and preaching partners either found them in prayer or in the bed. Oh how he wanted to go to bed and get some rest. But not yet, for this sermon was nowhere near finished.

Pastor Lee began to pace back and forth in his study, wondering what to do. He had no more vacation days to take this year and it was definitely too short a notice to get a quality supply minister for Sunday morning. No, he had to do it himself. But how when nothing he wrote looked, sounded, or felt right to him?

Suddenly his eyes caught a glimpse of an index card that had fallen by the bookcase. Stooping down to pick it up he saw that on the card he had written down the title to a sermon he heard preached by a famous preacher in the county a few years ago. Although the card was yellowed with age he could still just barely make out the notes he had taken.

"That was so long ago, I'm sure no one will ever know that this is not my own message" Lee thought. "After all, he probably got it from somebody else and Solomon did say "There is nothing new under the sun." I'm so tired I cannot keep my eyes open, let alone think straight!" With that thought in mind, Pastor Lee places the index card in his Bible at the appropriate new Scripture passage, turned off the lights and the television in his study, and walked across the hall to his bedroom for a brief night's sleep. Ready or not, Sunday was here.

Sound familiar? Maybe not to you, but to many ministers, pastors, preachers and evangelists around the world this scenario plays out more often than they would like to admit, even to themselves. Sunday has arrived and you know in your heart there Is no fresh manna from above. The cupboard is bare and the sermon bank is NSF...no sermon found! Might as well start to pack your bags for "Lower Flunkerville" for the trip will begin in just a few short hours.

Many preachers and pastors secretly fear that the day will come that after the sermonic selection has been sung, they will stand literally having nothing to say. Some admittedly have gone or are going through a dry spell. Wrestling with the Lord like Jacob, not wanting to let go until the Lord blesses our soul but still not seemingly receiving that "Word" we need in the morning. Still others unfortunately have sadly abandoned any pretense of study, preferring instead to glean from the crops others have harvested. Instead of sowing their own seeds of prayer and study, cultivating them by prayer and meditation, and weeding out the "bad growth" by prayer and research, they opt for the easy way out and steal something that never belonged to them in the first place.

I am talking about those that blatantly rip-off sermons from other preachers then pass them off as their own with no work at all. Sort of a generic one sermon fits all type mentality. Those who only buy sermons on tape only to copy them word for word and preach them one week later and have the audacity to declare to those they preach to that "The Lord gave this to me." Professionally speaking, the world would consider this to be plagiarism. In the preaching world, unfortunately for too many ministers it is called business as usual.

Plagiarism is aptly defined as "to steal and pass off as one's own, the ideas or words of another." (Websters 7th New Collegiate Dictionary pg. 646) It is noted that it is the **deliberate known transposing** of another's work, and **promoting it** as one's own work without giving proper credit and acknowledgment to the known original author. In the secular arena this often proves to be an untenable action as the ramifications, if discovered, could lead to revoking of accreditation, forfeiture of awards and or degrees if awarded based on the plagiarized work, along with the humiliation that would ultimately come with being branded a fraud by peers and co-workers.

However, how can we preachers possibly give proper credit to every prophet and preacher, every minister of God that has ever lived who might of spoken on the same subject. That same word that is tugging the strings of our soul shouting "Preacher please preach me!" How, when we will invariably end up with sermons that if enough investigation was done, we will find that someone, somewhere has preached the very same message with the very same central theme? Is it even possible to do as such when the Apostle Peter declares before the council that he and John could do no more (or no better!) than *"speak the things which we have seen and heard."* (Acts 4:20). Apostle Paul also affirms this position in Acts 26:22d *"saying none other thing than those things which the prophets and Moses did say should come."*

Every preacher gets both inspiration and information not only from the Holy Spirit and the Bible, but also from other ministers. To deny the very fact that other ministers have helped to open our eyes to different and sometimes difficult passages of Scriptures is facetious indeed. Two such passages of Scripture come to my mind in my own personal experience. One is Luke 7:32 and the other is Matthew 24:20. Although reading and researching both these Scriptures, I felt as if I did not have a firm enough grasp on them to deliver an intelligent message on either one. However after I heard two different ministers preach these texts, the Holy Spirit opened my eyes to see things that had previously been obscured from me. Though I still have yet to minister on these texts, I definitely have additional insights to glean from.

The problem is when a minister takes another's sermon and proceeds to preach the same message **verbatim;** without any personal prayer time, reflection, or insight, and then incorporate what the Holy Spirit is able to give them into that same message. I am not talking about building sermons from outlines that can be purchased and are published for that express purpose with the proper research and preparation. How do you know that the research on the paper you bought or the book you lifted that sermon from is correct, unless you research it yourself?

What would be the response of many of our congregations if they only knew that Pastor's last pew tipping, sister shouting, brother weeping sermon on last Sunday was not the result of the intense prayer life and the sanctified study sessions that they thought their pastor personally sacrificed, set aside and sought the Lord for? That quality time they were also paying for? Instead of following the lead of the Holy Spirit and listening to His guidance for the message for the morning, they rather relied on a purchased piece of paper (Neatly outlined, homiletically and hermeneutically precise, and perfectly alliterated of course) that they could buy at a conference or convention; or a "Saturday Night Special" from a fellow preacher. By the way, a "Saturday Night Special" is just what its name implies. It is a quick last minute research methodology by way of telephone, e-mail, or Internet on the Saturday night immediately before Sunday's proclamation. I am talking about the planned, deliberate using of another man or woman's entire sermon and passing it off as an original message hot off the prayer room presses and delivered straight from the Lord devoid of any part of you.

Much of our failure in the delivery of our sermons has to do with our lack of proper preparation. Like Pastor Lee above, we wait until the last minute and then hurriedly try to cut and paste something together and pray that nobody will notice. So much of our time is focused on so many other aspects of ministerial life that we rob the Lord of that special time to commune with us and we with Him. We need that time alone with God. When we do not get alone with God, we begin to lose the strength and substance of our Christ connection.

When our devotions diminish:

- Vision begins to vanish…
- Discipline lacks direction…
- Faith feels for facts…
- Possibility is pre-empted by problems…
- Foundations falter and fail…

- Hope is handcuffed
- Praise is prevented....
- Proclamation is powerless

My friend, Rev. K. Ed Copeland, Jr., JD from Kankakee, Illinois has shown both the importance and the interaction between our devotions and our delivery. He writes "Ideally, what you preach should be a distillation or at least a derivation of what God has been speaking to you about in your private devotions. That is one of the reasons maintaining a daily devotion is so vital to the ministry." [1]

It is the in the seedbed of our devotional life that God sows the seeds of revelation that eventually grow into sermons, only if they are nurtured, protected, cultivated and cared for. It is called preparation. Rev. Donald H. Bowen in his book *"Passing the Torch: Changing Church Leadership in a Changing World"* says of preparation "The disciplined pastor will find time to prepare challenging, inspiring messages for the people, and they (the people) have every right to expect this. People... will overlook many faults of the pastor, but they are not very forgiving of the pastor who constantly comes to the pulpit unprepared. Such preparation requires a lot of time, effort, energy and prayer. Seldom will a pastor have a valid excuse for not being prepared." [2]

It has been rightly said on many occasions that the people will forgive their pastors of many things. They will forgive them if they are not efficient and effective administrators. They will forgive them if they are not perfect parliamentarians. They will be forgiven if they are not community activists. The people will wink and nod when pastor sings in a key that challenges even the most versatile musician's creativity to save them from drowning. But the one thing that pastors, preachers, ministers, evangelists, et al, will not be forgiven for is the crime of not preaching. Good preaching, like good cooking must be prepared properly, seasoned subtly, and simmer slowly so that the meat falls from the bone.

Let it Grow before you Let it Go!

Proper sermon preparation is analogous to the various stages of childbirth. We are overcome and overjoyed at the culmination of the process but there is a wealth of learning to be gained from studying the diverse stages. We place so much energy, emphasis, and effort on the joy at the moment of delivery that we neglect to ensure proper care and caution of ourselves during the process of preparation. There is a process of development that must take place in your head, in your heart, and in your life more so than in your notes before you are ready to deliver any one particular message. Again, Copeland states "You cannot short circuit the process or you will give birth to an underdeveloped sermon." (3)

How many sermons have we delivered before they were ready to see the light of day? How many times have we just did a "drive by" exegesis coupled with a "hit and run" prayer? The Lord does not bless and we do not understand it. Many times we wonder why the praise is pathetic and the power prohibited in the House of the

Redeemed; where the remnant ought to be rejoicing in the realization of the revelation that God has been good to them! We blame the coldness of spirit, the hardness of heart, the internal idiosyncrasies of our people (they just don't get it) instead of humbly facing the fact that we just delivered a premature proclamation!

Anything that is birthed prematurely does not function at an optimum level. Children that are born premature not only have immediate struggles but impending setbacks. Things that you cannot always see on the outside can and often do affect one that is born prematurely for the rest of their lives. They suffer from an arrested development.

Sermons are much like children. That is why we resist and resent criticism and correction of the sermons we develop. If it was birthed in you, then it is a part of you. Even if your child goes astray, that is still your child. You and your spouse may talk about them in negative tones but you will not let anyone else do so. That is the way we treat our sermons. Even if it failed to produce the result we intended, we may talk about our own. But you would not dare let another person or preacher do the same.

4

An Analysis And Application

*"Make your ear attentive to wisdom, incline your heart
to understanding; For if you cry for discernment, lift your
voice for understanding; if you seek her as silver, and
search for her as hidden treasures; Then you will discern
the fear of the Lord and discover the knowledge of God."*
Proverbs 2:2-5 NAS

In observing the stages of the birthing process of my
children, the Lord revealed to me that several of the
identifiable stages of childbirth have some intrinsic
crossover value. They can be readily applied to the discipline of properly preparing to preach the Word of
God. However, it does not deal with the entirety of the
process of putting together the sermon yet. For now
we will just deal with the seed that has been sown.
How well the scripture reminds us

*"We were pregnant, we writhed in labor, we gave birth
as it were, only to wind...."* (Isaiah 26:18 NAS)

Communicating Your Passion

"Every tree is known by its fruit." (St. Luke 6:44)

Seed that is sown in good ground; that is properly nurtured and cared for will bear fruit. A seed is not planted to remain a seed, but to break forth from its slumber and rise, breaking forth through the hardness of the earth. Stretching towards the radiant sun and welcoming the rains it grows and eventually bears fruit. This analysis prepares us to begin to formulate a process of organization and structure of a sermon, to ensure that the seed that has been sown in your spirit reaches maturity. Keeping our mind, focused then on the task at hand let us observe the stages of childbirth.

Ovulation - The release of a mature ovum (egg) from an ovary. Every month the woman releases an egg from her ovaries as it (the egg) prepares to meet and receive the sperm and thus become fertilized. The egg travels through the fallopian tubes with plans of planting itself on the wall of the uterus. This is the seed that is already in the spirit of the preacher. The particular way in which an issue or idea hits you like it does no one else. Whether from your own private and personal experiences, reading good books that challenge and stimulate your mind, or through a time of sharing with trusted clergy friends, this seed is only in you. However we cannot rush to the pulpit yet, for the time to release this inspirational thought (that is all it really is at this point) is not yet.

Fertilization - The union of an ovum (egg) and a sperm to produce a single cell (zygote) that then develops into an embryo. In order to be fertilized the sperm must enter the seed in order for conception to occur. More precisely it must penetrate before it can be proclaimed that one is pregnant. It does not matter how **much semen** is present, it is **the sperm** that causes the egg to change from just an egg to a zygote, and determines the sex of the child. The Spirit of God must possess that seed that is within you if it is going to grow to a full-fledged sermon. In fact it must penetrate to the core of the seed if we are to truly give a God given message.

If the Spirit of the Lord does not penetrate the seed then we cannot rightly proclaim that the Lord is the "Father" of this sermon or the giver of the life to the seed. If He is not the "Father" then He has no responsibility to protect, or provide for whatever is birthed from us.

Gestation - The time from conception to birth. Premature births happen in this time period. This is a time of both necessary and crucial development. Care must be taken to ensure that one eats healthy, gets plenty of rest, and eliminates anything that could harm the development of the child or stress the body to the point that we can no longer carry the child and he/she will either be born premature or aborted. In sermon development care must be taken to ensure that the sermon will be properly developed. Do not rush the sermon to market. There is a set time of God given delivery that I believe varies from preacher to preacher. For some it may be a two weeks, for others some months, others a year or more and still others may only take a couple of days. Regardless of how it works with you, the sermon ought to be developed properly. Do not preach it until it is. So if that means holding off a couple of weeks from preaching it until it has traveled through all these various stages, then let it be. It will be worth the wait. Ask any parent.

Maturation - When the fetus has fully developed and is ready for delivery. Development is as complete as it can be in the womb. All organs are functioning properly, blood tests have come back positive, heartbeat is strong, the identification of the baby as a male or female is more accurate. Labor pains begin. Final preparations are made to prepare for the moment of delivery. This is the time of impending joy. Excitement is building. The journey is almost completed. The seed has matured into a sermon. We feel it. It gives us pleasure to be so close with this life that God has birthed in us and entrusted to our care. It has been developed properly, well nurtured and all looks favorable for a successful delivery.

All we want to know is "when will it be over, when can I preach this sermon" and just as important "where will this sermon be delivered at?" Sometimes we forget that just like a child, the sermon should be delivered in the best circumstances possible. In other words you should know where the Lord told you to birth this sermon. It may not be "County Hospital," "Rural Retreat," "City Care Complex" or "Mountain Memorial." It may not be your home church, or the church you pastor, or the last night of revival. We must constantly seek the Lord to make sure that we are preaching the right word at the right time for the right people and in the right situation.

Position - This is when the child begins the turning process in the womb to a "head downward" position to finalize for the preparation of birth. Labor pains begin and increase in frequency and intensity the closer that we get to the moment of delivery. Still we must hold on just a little while longer. We are so close! If the transition stage is not completed successfully, this may lead to a breech birth or a caesarian section due to the child being tangled around the   umbilical cord. Sunday is coming! The date is set. You are more ready to preach now than you have ever been before in your life. This is more than just another sermon. This sermon has come alive kicking you, wanting to get out. You can feel it.

This one will be a "house wrecker, a masterpiece, a horse you can ride anywhere, a dog that will hunt even on a rainy day." The words are leaping off the paper. Your spirit is overwhelmed within you as you marvel at what the Lord has done. But hold on just a little while. Take a little time to thank the Lord and meditate on what He has given you to share with His people. Preach it to yourself several times before you preach it to God's people once. He has entrusted you with the task of bringing forth His word in the manner He has given you. That is enough right there to make you slow down just enough to ensure a smooth transition from the head and the heart to the hearers. Too many great sermons have been lost from the study to the pulpit. Or once they are birthed they do not look at all like what was developed. Why? We simply pushed just a little too soon and celebrated way too early.

Transition and Completion – Delivery day has come! The great moment of a new life being birthed into this world. Labor pains will soon cease. The womb opens up. This is the time for the big push. No time to be cute. Down through the canal the child comes. Next to the joy of being saved, there is no joy greater that I know of than the birth of a child. When it is all over and that child is placed in your arms; as you hold him or her in your hands and witness the mystery of life, you Thank God on one hand for life and thank God again that it (the pregnancy) is over on the other hand. The time for the delivery of that which has been birthed in you has come. Now it is time to bring forth your seed turned sermon for the world to see. No time to be cute or to try to impress folks. It is time to P.U.S.H! (pray until something happens) Realize that the devil does not want this seed to see the light of day. Too much is at stake to be nonchalant. Too many lives will be blessed. Too many strongholds will be broken. Generational curses will be bound by the authority of the Son of God. Lives must be and will be changed when the Word of the Lord is preached!

It is not about making them shout but about planting that same seed that has been sown in us into their lives so that it may transform their lives. Do not let the adversary strangle the life out of this seed so that it is stillborn.

Celebration - A cry. A sign of life. That which has been carried in us is now outside of us. The baby is whisked away for a check of all vital signs. All extremities are checked for any abnormalities. Pain gives way to pleasure as our seed, our child, our heir is named. It is all over now.

Time for the nurturing to begin. With a clear understanding as to what should occur at each stage of the preparation, we now move forward to the development of a prayerful and purposeful process.

Notes on Section 2 Chapter 4

1. K. Ed. Copeland, JD, Riding in the Second Chariot, pg # 21 PrayerCloset Publishing 1999
2. Donald H. Bowen, "Passing the Torch," pg# 86 Sonrise Press 1998
3. Copeland, pg # 21
4. All medical definitions are taken from "The World Book Medical Encyclopedia Copyright 1988 World Book Inc., Chicago, Il.

Section III

Process

"Let the words of my mouth, and the meditation of my heart, be acceptable in thy sight, O Lord, my strength, and my redeemer."
Psalms 19:14

There was a young preacher who had accepted the pastorate of a fine and upstanding church in the heart of the city. Although this would be his first pastoral charge, he came well prepared for the task that was at hand. He possessed a solid education. All of his degrees from upper echelon universities were proudly displayed on the wall of his study. His references were impeccable, having been written by some of the most regarded pastors around the country. His internship was served at a church where the pastor was considered to be one of the greatest preachers in the state. On name recognition alone many preachers were given major opportunities to preach and pastor simply because this well-established Pastor had requested it. He was the youngest pastor not only in the history of the church but in the city as well. The church paid him well enough that with some creative budgeting it was enough to take care of both him and his wife so that she did not have to work.

This neophyte pastor soon let his blessing go to his head. He became arrogant, cocky, a little too self-assured. He began to spend his days "making contacts," rubbing shoulders with the movers and shakers in town, and offering the invocation at various council meetings. Nights were filled with meetings, "showing his face" at revivals and conferences. He made every major meeting, hearing and committee session because he did not have to work another job. After all he was the "Senior Pastor" of City Church, Inc. If he did not show up to these meetings to represent "his church" then he would make his church look bad. With what they were paying him, he could not afford to let that happen.

Predictably the quality of his sermons began to suffer. He quickly exhausted his supply of sermons that he had developed while he was searching for a church to pastor. He began to revamp and re-circulate sermons hoping that no one would notice. Like many ministers he thought he could get by on God, grace, and his gifts. He began to openly brag and flaunt the fact that he did not have to study but so much. His seminary training could be quickly recalled and it did not make sense to waste so much precious time studying; especially when he felt that people could not appreciate what he was saying if he did.

Eventually this got around to the Deacon board who had noticed that his sermons had fallen off a bit. Genuinely concerned, they asked to meet with him, to see if there was anything that they could do to ease his workload if necessary. After devotions, the chairman gently asked if there was any way that the deacons could help him, so that he could devote more time to his study.

"Brother Deacon," the pastor replied, "I do not need any help as I see it. I am representing the church across a variety of important community organizations. We are standing tall in the sight of our ecclesiastical sister churches. The messages that I bring are specifically tailored to reach as many worshippers as possible on Sunday morning."

"But Pastor, how much time are you able to dedicate your study of the Word of God?"

The Pastor responded "Well, my training has served me well, I think. I have cultivated a keen sense of what the inspired text is saying. Therefore, I just let the Lord tell me what to say to you and usually I prepare the message on Sunday morning. It is always in the back of my mind. But I do not start to bring it all together until Sunday. From the time I leave the front door of the parsonage to the time that I arrive at the front door of the church, I let God tell me what to tell you. That way there are no distractions that will deter me from saying what the Lord would have me to speak."

"I see," the chairman replied. "I think I know how we can help you now, Pastor."

At the next scheduled conference meeting when the time came for the Deacon's Board report, the Chairman stood up.

"Beloved of God, the Deacon's Board is concerned that our Pastor does not have enough time to study the Word. We met with him to see how we could better serve him, so that he could free himself from some of these temporal affairs. After talking with him and trying to understand how he manages his time, we have come up with a perfect solution. Therefore, we recommend that we purchase another parsonage **twenty miles away,** so that he can have more time to study."

Am I on your street?

Every minister has a process of developing a sermon. Right or wrong, good or bad. Regardless of how labor intensive or scant it may be. One may research a text and related materials for weeks or one may just scan a passage briefly with the proverbial "wing and a prayer." Yet we all have a process of putting sermons together. However you do, whatever you do is your personal process.

This is usually the nuts and bolts of many homiletic books. Tell me how to do it and hurry up because Sunday's sermon cannot wait. We want an easy fix and solution to the problem at hand. We want every sermon to be a Ken Griffey, Jr. homerun, Michael Jordan buzzer beater, or a Deion Sanders punt return for a touchdown to win the game. Yet we forget that statistics show that "Junior" strikes out more than he hits them out of the park, Jordan did not win every game with his last minute heroics, and Sanders cannot and does not break away all the time, much to the chagrin of his numerous fans.

By the Divine Providence of the Lord there is no easy formula for success. There is no proverbial "holy grail" that once found will make every sermon a masterpiece that even your pastor and/or mentor in the ministry wished they had preached it first. There will be as many "flunkers and clunkers" as there will be "masterpieces in the making." The blessing of God is those sermons that we feel are worthy of being entered into the "Flunkerville Hall of Fame" are the usually and uniquely the same sermons that seem to have the most profound and positive effect on the people who hear them. How well can we witness with Paul:

"But we have this treasure in earthen vessels, that the excellency of the power may be of God and not of us."
(II Corinthians 4:7)

Preparing to preach, the process of putting it together and preaching in general is hard work. There is no way around it. You must be prepared to sweat. You must be prepared to wrestle like Jacob, make war like David and be wise like Solomon. There is an axiom that declares "If you would aspire to greatness you must be prepared to perspire the greatest." This is not only in preaching but in life as well.

While in no means does this chapter cover every possible and conceivable area in the discipline of putting together passionate Biblically sound sermons, this does serve as a platform for personal review. There are many wonderful books that I have referenced or included in the bibliography in the back of this book. I highly recommend them to you.

5

The Forgotten Disciplines

"And Jesus answered and said unto her, "Martha, Martha thou art careful and troubled about many things: But one thing is needful: and Mary has chosen that good part, which shall not be taken away from her."
St. Luke 10:41-42

There are four areas of concern that quite often do not get enough attention from too many preachers. These neglected and needful disciplines affect not only the quality and passion of one's preaching, but one's personal growth as well. If our personal spiritual growth is stunted, then we will deliver spiritually stunted sermons. It is impossible to effectively develop something for others that has not been developed (I did not say perfected) in you first.

Prayer Life

We must develop a regular and consistent prayer life. To say that we are preachers of the Lord's gospel without participating in the discipline of prayer causes us to understand why our preaching has so little power. We speak forth words of Life that are stillborn because they have not been pushed down the birthing canal of prayer. Andrew Murray writes "Lord teach us to pray. Yes to pray. This is what we need to be taught. Though in its simplest beginnings prayer is so simple that the feeblest child can pray, yet it is at the same time the highest and holiest work to which man can rise. It is fellowship with the Unseen and the Most Holy One. The powers of the eternal world have been placed at its disposal. It is the very essence of true religion, the channel of all blessings, the secret of power and life." (1)

The Bible points to the Lord as hearing our prayers even before we utter them!

Before they call I will answer; while they are still speaking I will hear. (Isaiah 65:24 NIV)

The Lord hears the prayers of the righteous. (Proverbs 15:29 NIV)

For the eyes of the Lord are on the righteous and her ears are attentive to their prayer. (I Peter 3:12 NIV)

Our prayer life must not only subsist of a thirty second grace before meals (some would say that is too long), a quick "Thank you, Jesus" for making it through the day, and the ever present "Have mercy Lord" because we have not prepared ourselves properly to preach on Sunday. Hoping that God will accept these expressive exclamations as sincere petitions of faith and trust in Him is to assuredly play with God.

Devotionals

It is an absolute necessity to set quiet time alone with God. Much has already been said about this discipline. I would recommend that the preacher keep a seed book. In it, write down things that the Lord reveals to you during your devotional time. This is the perfect time to read your way through that book on faith that you bought at the Christian bookstore that is gathering dust on your shelves. Resist the temptation and do not try to develop these notes into a sermon. There will be plenty of time for that later on. If you begin to put sermons together during your devotional time, you are shortchanging yourself in this meaningful aspect of your relationship with the Lord. This will serve as a grace garden of ideas that may be cultivated at a later date.

Pastor/Mentor

Every pastor needs a pastor. We need someone that we can and will be accountable to. Someone that has been where we have been and who is ministering at the level or higher than we aspire to be. The tragic negligence of this one area of discipline has left many ministers floundering without a lifejacket in a sea of clergy killers.

Every minister needs a faithful, Bible Based, Christ Centered, Spirit Filled and Life Related Pastor who will lovingly take them under their wings - regardless of whether or not they were birthed directly through their ministry - and impart their wisdom and spirit into those who shall catch the mantle when it falls. There is no success without successors.

Every Timothy and Titus needs a Paul.
Every Elisha needs an Elijah.
Every John Mark needs both a Paul and a Barnabus.

Success breeds Success

In the Gospel of Luke, we discover Mary receiving the news of her being the vessel through which the Messiah shall be born from the angel Gabriel. Then he tells her that her cousin Elizabeth is with child as well and in her six month of pregnancy. Notice that the angel does not tell Mary to visit her cousin. There is no revelation in the inspired text that she received commandment from Jehovah to go and check on Elizabeth. Yet scripture clearly reveals that Mary made haste to be with Elizabeth and abode there for three months.

I do not believe that Mary was going simply to be inquisitive. It was more than the fact that she was **concerned for the condition of her cousin** but in reality she was **compelled for the cause of the Creator**. As long as Mary hung around home, there was a greater chance that she would not hold onto what she had heard from the angel. But by being with Elizabeth, she was around somebody who was in the process of birthing her own blessing. Surely that had to encourage Mary. If her cousin could be blessed in her advanced years then certainly she could be blessed too.

Like Mary we must learn to hang out with blessed folks if we want to learn how to be strong enough to birth a blessing in our ministries when the time is right. While we should not discriminate against any minister (regardless of school attendance, fraternity, size of church currently serving, etc.) we should definitely want to hang our proverbial hats with those who are blessed like we desire to be blessed. They can teach us the principles that the Lord has taught them. We can set our house in order and do preventative maintenance so that we will be ready if and when the Lord moves us elsewhere. We can receive encouragement when things get rough from someone who has "Been there, Done that, and Survived by the Power of God!"

Ministers, like the people we preach to, can pull us down into the valley of despair and depression with them. Because they never achieved much in the ministry, they attempt to convince others that we should not even try to do much more than preach and pick up the check. They never became a full-time pastor with a full time salary as opposed to a salary that requires the minister to be bi or tri-vocational, so then we should just be satisfied where we are and never hope, pray, or plan for things to change. The old saying is true that "Misery loves company."

Not every Pastor is a mentor. Every pastor does not want other ministers to see him or her as they really are. This is in no way a discredit to, or a disclaimer against supporting your pastor or to insinuate that they are living contrary to the will and Word of God. Honor and bless your pastor at all times, regardless of how they treat you. You will be blessed through your faithfulness.

A mentor is one that you would want to pattern your life and ministry after. They are a trusted counselor or a guide. Some Pastors do not fill that role and are very uncomfortable in doing so. Others could only mentor you in how to be as unethical and underhanded as they are. Still others can take you to a point or a certain level in the ministry and then they too must pass the torch to someone who can take you to the next level in your spiritual maturity. Pastors with the right type of spirit will not be jealous or intimidated by the fact that God is taking you to ministry on a different level than they currently are. They will want to help you anyway that they can, even if it means letting you go ahead of them.

Ask the Lord to reveal to you whom He wants to be your mentor. Pray and ask God's guidance. If He reveals your present Pastor, make an appointment and talk with them about it. They might just be willing. If not, or if the Lord reveals someone else, contact whomever the Lord reveals. They may not be the best preacher in town or pastor the largest church in the city. They may not have all the connections that you think they should have to get you where you want to go. But if the Lord reveals them to you and confirms it through His word, then be faithful to God. **Do not leave your church under any circumstances unless God specifically tells both you and your Pastor that this is what you are to do if you are to be found in the will of God.** Again, if your Pastor has the right type of Spirit they will want to a blessing to your ministry however they can.

If you would be a Mentor...

A mentor must be accessible and available. Some Pastors are just too busy to be effective mentors. Some never return phone calls, pages, or e-mails. Some happily accept your money to be a part of their movement and under their covering but insist you have to track them down for they are far too busy to be bothered with every preacher that wants their help, or just wants to talk. While for some that may be the sign of a successful Pastor, it could just as well indicate a Pastor with bad time management or one that neglects their own church to preach at everyone else's church. Leaving messages on voice mail that never get returned or sending e-mails that never get answered have a crippling effect on a minister that is sincerely seeking help from an experienced elder minister. As quiet as it is kept, many ministers suffer with a spirit of rejection and crave to be appreciated and accepted. Sometimes we unintentionally add to that sense of rejection when we do not return phone calls for two to three weeks.

I have seen a marked rise of associate ministers leaving major churches (with a cadre of associate ministers) and joining smaller churches (with two or perhaps three associates at the most) so that they could be a little closer to the pastor as a mentor. They often found themselves lost in the shuffle in some of the larger ministries and never seemed to be able to really catch up to the Pastor but on Sunday morning, if they were fortunate. Their experience was one likened to a bakery or doctor's office where you take a number and wait in line please.

A mentor must know how to be both open and closed for business at the same time. They must be open and mature enough to let the cracks show in their life. Let others see the wounded healer. Do not be afraid to show your scrapes, scars, and scabs. Be extremely careful about who you decide to be accountable to. Do not let any pastor or minister that desires you to be "their son or the heir of their ministry" simply so they can boast about the number of ministers that they have under them to put pressure on you to join their church. If the Lord has sanctioned it, then they will be willing to wait on God's timing. If not and you jump ahead of the Lord you are just asking for trouble.

Mentors must know how to keep the privacy of the confessional sacred. We should hold all personal information that is shared with us a trust from God. It is both unwise and unethical to share another Pastors' problems with another minister, even if all three are mutual friends. Things that are shared in confidence should never see the light of day. There are issues that our members reveal to us that are so sensitive that we would never reveal them to another, or even to our spouses. However, it seems like when it comes to the same type of private information coming from our pastoral and preaching peers, nothing is off limits. How much information have we shared with someone that we honestly felt would not reveal it (wife, partner, hunting buddy, etc.) that they shared it with one of their close peers and so on. When it is all revealed who gets the blame and who feels miserable. You do if you broke that confidence.

A Word of Warning!

Not everyone can handle this type of relationship! You must be led by the Spirit of God to discover whom you can safely trust to be your mentor and your preaching confidant. It may even be better to limit what information that you share until the Lord confirms that they can be trusted. Not every preacher and pastor wants to see you blessed and prosper. Not every pastor wants to see you pastor. Not every schoolmate wants to see you get the major city church with a wonderful package while they have been stuck in the rural church far longer than they had ever fathomed, struggling to make ends meet. They may turn any negativity in your life into an advantage for them. Many preachers have been circumvented in the field of the pastorate by other ministers that had or found out from other preachers' "dirt" on them and wanted the same pastorate for themselves or their "frat, clique, co-worker, or seminary" partner. Regardless of the risks, you still need somebody to be your mentor.

Comprehensive Study

This is more than just proofreading a text to piece together next week's sermon. This must be a disciplined and determined effort to wrestle with the things of faith. This is the time to thoroughly research whatever subject the Lord lays on your heart. The preacher must set aside a consistent study time each day. If at all possible it should be at the same time each day. Certainly, no less than one hour a day should be spent simply in studying the Word of God.

Take the time to thoroughly investigate through the Bible the various doctrines and disciplines of the Word of God. How does your personal faith square with what you have learned? What is the church's position concerning your area of study? Study the lives of the apostles and prophets. How do their lives mark and mirror yours? When was the last time that you did a detailed biblical analysis on the covenants of the Bible, characteristics and attributes of God, the law of the offerings, marriage or church growth? We are quick to grab hold to what another "famous" minister may say about a subject and preach it without even checking it out for ourselves. What if they made a mistake? You will never know until you study it for yourself.

"Study to shew thyself approved unto God, a workman

that needeth not to be ashamed, rightly dividing the word of truth." (II Timothy 2:15)

Keep a study notebook handy. This is not your seed bed book. This is where you will keep a detailed record of your study times, texts, topics, and thoughts. It is here that you will contend for the faith as you search for the will of God in your life and rightly divide the word of truth. Write your notes out.

To aid your study you will need some additional tools. By no means is this an exhaustive list but it should serve to give you a good understanding of various topics and issues in the Bible.

A. Study Bible(s)
B. Several Bible translations.
C. Hebrew/Greek Lexicon
D. Bible Dictionary
E. A good commentary
F. Dictionary
G. A good Concordance

If you find yourself too busy for this amount of study, then you are too busy. Re-order your schedule and become a better manager of your time. Dr. Harold A. Carter, Sr., Senior Pastor of New Shiloh Baptist Church in Baltimore, Maryland warns the preacher that would be lazy. He writes "Laziness always tries to cover itself by turning stones into bread. It circumvents hard work, ignores creative abilities, and uses itself to fool people. 'Preparation for preaching is plowing the mind, turning it over so that fresh growth may appear. It is a long furrow. But whoever puts his hand to the plow and is not willing to go on to the end, with taut physical and mental muscles and a determined grip on the plow handles, is not worthy of the ministry." (2)

6

Selecting a Text

"Come and hear, all ye that fear God, and I will declare what He hath done for my soul."
Psalms 66:15

The time has come for us to finally begin to put the sermon together. Where will we ever begin? **Down on our knees!** If we would remember to call on the Savior and construct the appropriate structure for our sermon then we will be better able to craft the sermon.

If one has been diligent in their prayer life, devotional time and study time, I believe that they will have sufficient resources to get started with. Sermons are all around you. Keep your eyes and ears open to observe what is going on in your world and ask God what His Holy Word has to say about it. The ministers of the Lord will always have a Word from God if they have been faithful in their task of preparing themselves to be obedient to God as they tarry in His presence. It may not fit your preferred manner or blueprint for preaching but it will be the right word for the right time.

If one is negligent in their personal study, however, sermon time will leave them struggling to look for the nearest quick fix they can find. The refrain from the past is true: "Nothing from nothing leaves nothing." You cannot pull out of you anything that has not been planted within you. This one failure has caused the proliferation of instant sermon books, pamphlets, websites (www.hoophelp.now or www.needaword.asap) and other escape hatches to make up for a lack in the study of the Word of the Lord. There is a definite difference in using these study aids to assist your study early in the process in an area or on a topic as opposed to replacing your study.

I am a firm believer of being ahead of schedule if at all possible. There are emergencies that will come up from time to time to throw you off track. However, if one can be prepared ahead of time, it reduces the stress and worry of what to preach and allows one to perhaps better focus on how to preach what God has given them to preach. My friend, Rev. Leroy Armstrong of Louisville, Kentucky taught a class on expository preaching for the Virginia Baptist State Convention. During that class, he instructed us to get two weeks ahead as far as our sermon preparation. He was not just alluding to what you think or feel that you are going to preach but to literally have the sermon written and ready. Good advice to heed.

This also provides a mechanism for preventing the mismatching of topics with texts that do not support the thought of the text. We may produce a great title but in our rush to get it "to market" we will proofread the first seemingly applicable text that we find, even if it has to be taken out of its scriptural context to make it work. This is often because we are rushing the process of development because we are behind schedule instead of ahead of it. By getting two weeks ahead, there is no rush deadline.

There has to be a Reason!

No sermon should be preached simply because it is Sunday and they have to hear something. You ought to be able to intelligently state the purpose of the message. If the message has no purpose then you are like a hunter trying to kill a deer at a great distance with a shotgun as opposed to a rifle. The greater the distance of the shot, (beyond 40 yards) the greater chance that you will miss your target, even though you can see it. The shot will spread out over a greater area, thereby only grazing what you had intended to kill. A rifle, however, is honed for a truer shot, although you still must be able to see what you are aiming at.

Too many sermons fall short of our expectations because we are either trying to hit them at a distance, or our aim is off. A defined purpose statement for each and every sermon helps the preacher to focus on what they believe the Lord wants them to address in that particular message.

In developing the purpose, you must produce a methodology of developing how you reach your conclusion or purpose. If your purpose is to lead the church into spiritual maturity in the area of forgiveness, how do you propose to do that? How are you going to take the people where the Lord has just brought you? How did you arrive at this purpose statement?

In *The Witness of Preaching*, Thomas G. Long makes some excellent formulas or sermon forms for arriving at your declared purpose that will be revealed through the homiletic pursuit. They are briefly as follows:

- If this….then this… and thus this.
- This is true in this way… and also in thus way, and in this other way too.
- This is the problem… this is the response of the gospel… these are the implications.
- This is the promise of the gospel. Here is how we can live out that promise.
- This is the historical situation in the text… these are the meanings for us now.
- Not this… or this… or this… or this… but this.
- Here is a prevailing view but here is the claim of the gospel.
- This… but what about this? …well, then this… yes, but what about that?
- Here is a story.
- Here is a letter.
- This? … or that? Both this and that. (3)

Which comes First?

Topic or text? Text or topic? Which one should the preacher identify first before they begin the process of putting the sermon together? The topic of the sermon must be related to the text. Mismatching topics with texts happen often, and it usually occurs when one is rushing to put something together.

While I believe that the majority of ministers started first with a topic and then found a text when they first started preaching, a great majority of preachers are now starting by selecting the text first and sticking to the text. This is a preferred method of text selection. They would consider themselves to be expository preachers. Expository in their development of the sermon if not necessarily in the delivery of the sermon. Dr. Robert Houston, Senior Pastor at the New Hope Friendship Missionary Baptist Church of San Diego, California gives the associate ministers that the Lord has entrusted to him ten reasons for expository preaching. These were developed by the E. K. Bailey Conference on Expository Preaching, They are:

1. Expository preaching creates a Bible bringing congregation.
2. Expository preaching creates a Bible loving congregation.
3. Expository preaching creates a Word conscious congregation.
4. Expository preaching forces the preacher to proclaim the whole counsel of God.

5. Expository preaching arms the people for spiritual warfare.

6. Expository preaching meets the needs of the people, which never occur to the preacher.

7. Expository preaching engenders tremendous interest in upcoming sermons.

8. Expository preaching challenges the life of the preacher.

9. Expository preaching allows the people to hear God's words and not the preachers' thoughts.

10. Expository preaching establishes the authority of God's word as opposed to situational ethics. (4)

Keep a notebook of topics that the Lord gives you. Write them done at once. If not, you may just lose that topic for many years. In your study time research both the wording of the topic and any appropriate scriptures. Do not try to force it to work. The sermon may develop into a topical sermon (even if you do not think that is your strength) giving you many different scriptures to draw from that will biblically support your topic.

I prefer to do the exegesis of the text and let the text tell me the topic. It is not only true that good meat makes its own gravy; but if it is cooked right it will fall from the bone. A quality study reaps so many rewards that I may work on topic and text assignments early in the week for a limited time. If the Lord reveals a connection, I put it on the drawing board to work on. If not, I am not rushed, because my study of the text that God gives will reveal the topic, and I am one week ahead of schedule if not two weeks.

Planning your days

Those who fail to plan, plan to fail. The preacher must have a systematic way of preparing their sermons. Once the structure of study has been crafted, it provides a template for their pursuit of preaching excellence. To avoid scenarios like our fictitious Pastor Lee in the section on Preparation, we must adhere to a set study time and format. The time spent preparing to preach could be set aside in the following manner.

Monday

Day of rest.

After preaching two or three sermons a Sunday, the body needs to rest. There are some within the ministerial community that feel like this is the perfect day and opportunity to study hard since they perceive that they are more attuned and open to the Spirit of the Lord. However, I choose this day as one to rest and relax. In addition, this is the perfect day for me to spend quality time with myself - to relax and unwind. No books, tapes, magazines or church related telephone calls. The members in the church know that Monday is Pastor's day. If it is not an absolute emergency that no one but the Pastor can handle, it will not be dealt with on this day.

We must not feel guilty about taking time off to rest. If we do not rest properly our body will invariably break down. Stress, ulcers, heart attacks, high blood pressure, strokes, depression and so many other ailments can either be triggered by or made worse if we do not take time to rest. Jesus taught his disciples by His own personal example after a season of particularly challenging and successful ministries outreach the importance of getting away.

"And He said unto them, 'Come ye yourselves apart into a desert place and rest awhile': for there were many coming and going, and they had no leisure so much as to eat." (St. Mark 6:31)

If God took a day to rest, so should we. If Jesus took time to go into the desert away from everybody and rest, we as ministers must realize if that which is Spirit takes time to rest, then that which is flesh must also take time to rest.

Tuesday

Bible reading, creative brooding, and rough outline

This is the day to do your Bible reading, text and topic assignments, and to do some creative brooding over the proposed text to preach from. Take the time to think about it yourself, without rushing to pick up what somebody else more famous may have said about the same text. I firmly believe that God when He commissions us to this work has put within us an eye and a feel for the inspired text that He has not given anyone else.

Why would the Lord want or need a carbon copy of what He has already created? When you suppress what He has put in you in favor of that famous preacher that you are trying to emulate; what the Lord has put in you to give to the world dies. You only begin to see a text as Dr._____ would see it and deliver it like Pastor_____. You become a "mini me" version of the preacher, Pastor, Dean, Bishop, Professor, Televangelist, Evangelist or whoever you are trying so desperately to be like. Nobody can beat you at being you. If I had to go to Flunkerville, I would rather go to Flunk City being myself, than go trying to be somebody else.

Think creatively about the text. J. Grant Howard in *Creativity in Preaching,* echoes this thought. Although not speaking directly about the act of preaching but rather changing the climate in the local church for creative preaching, however these words have crossover application to the task of preparing sermons as well. He writes "Roots become ruts. Ruts become routines. Routine.........becomes righteous. Righteous routine becomes unassailably, uncritically rigid." (5)

Do not be afraid to let God speak to you through the text. Turn it as a diamond glistening in the light of the noon day sun. Turn it. Admire the nuances of the language. Discover the unusual points in usual proclamations. See it through the lens of your own experiences. Answer the questions: who, what, where, when, why, how, and perhaps the most important one of all how does this relate to me?

Feel free to do some light research on these things now. They will be fleshed out on tomorrow. Create a rough outline of ideas or issues that you feel are relevant to the text. Write them down.

Wednesday

Commentaries, Lexicons, and Tighten focus.

The day for exegesis is here. Fred Craddock, Professor of New Testament and Preaching at the Candler School of Theology, Emory University writes "The value of a commentary, as with any other resource, lies not only in the book itself but also in the point of the interpretive process at which the commentary is used. Introduce it too soon or too late into the process and the worth of even the best of books is sharply reduced." (6)

Vines and Shaddix define the process of exegesis in four parts: **Instigation, investigation, interpretation,** and **implication.** (7) There is nothing that will weed out flights of fancy and idiotic ideas better than good exegesis. Many great ideas have to be shelved when examined under the light of cautious and critical research of the text. Read what the commentators have written, keeping in mind that you too are a commentator. Those items that leap up at you take the time to do a little more research. Do not accept what Phillips, Henry, Clarke, Vines, Wiersbe or any others have written at face value alone. You must wrestle through it with prayer.

This is also the day for your word studies. Examine each word in its original context both in the original language and in its translation. Notice the interplay and interaction of the words together. Is this the only time it is used in the Bible? Where else? Take a good look at the unusual wording and punctuation as well. Several good points can be made off the unspeakable "Selah" or a well-placed comma or exclamation mark.

If one has access to the Internet or will admit that they have hiding in their personal "home" study several "Preaching made Simple or Oft Used Outlines" study books, this would be the day to cast a clandestine glance at them. I am not against help for we all need it sometimes. I just feel we should not rely on these ready-made resources as much as we do. This is the perfect day to see what your favorite preacher has to say on the text you that propose to preach from or to scan the Internet for a fresh focus. Be careful though! Remember that your congregation also scans the Internet and they do not just check their e-mail!

By now your preaching notebook or legal pad should have several pages of good information to glean from. Now it is time to begin to pinpoint exactly where you believe the Lord is leading you. Begin to organize this information into manageable piles of information: introduction, body, conclusion. illustrations, supporting scriptures, transitions (bridges), principles and points. We will not finalize the points today, just jot down some ideas.

Thursday

Develop points or principles with Scriptural backupand appropriate support structure.

We want to sharpen our sermon and give structure by identifying the main thoughts of the sermon. These are called either points or principles. **Points** are the truths that are found within the text that one proposes to preach from.

They may only be found in that text. **Principles** however are the truths that those same points teach that has a consistent application through both the scripture and in life. Whether one preaches points or principles, they should be able to support either in the Word of God. If it cannot be supported you are standing on shaky ground.

One may identify their points in any number of ways. Some tell the points, then teach the points one by one, then conclude by retelling the same points that were introduced and taught. Some may identify them either numerically or alphabetically. Some develop sub points beneath each point that support the main point. Still others develop their main thoughts and use them as they are.

Some identify their main points and sub points through a technique of reiterative patterns called alliteration or assonance. **Alliteration** is identifying the main words of the point by using the same letter. **Assonance** is identifying those same words with a similar sound, especially in its ending. (ism, tion, sion, ing, an, etc.) This manner of identifying the points or principles in a sermon greatly aids in the memorization of it and helps the hearer catch your main thought in a concise, effective phrase to help them identify the same truths that you have discovered for yourself.

In *The 12 Essential Skills for Great Preaching*, Wayne McDill writes "A sermon will be better grasped and remembered if the titles of its points have some sort of correspondence. They may have a similarity in sound, or in the first letter....Such devices may seem fatuous, but even the best speakers use them because they can make the difference between a speech being lost and its being followed and remembered." (8)

I have not identified any such examples here because there are several throughout the book. I use alliteration and assonance frequently, although I did not start using it when I became a minister. I have used this form in my youth writing poetry and as a teenager writing rap. I fell in love with the way the words sounded when used in this structure. Amazingly when I started preaching I did not use alliteration or assonance knowingly in sermons until I had been preaching about five years. Both the pastor who baptized me and nurtured me in the faith until I was a young adult and the pastor who licensed me in the gospel ministry did not use alliteration or assonance, so I did not even recognize its value in sermon structure until many years later.

Points or principles do not necessarily have to be alliterated. As long as they make good solid biblical and spiritual sense, they are fine. **Do not sacrifice the sound of the point for the substance of the point.** If the Lord gave it to you it will work. Whatever the points or principles that you desire to preach, make sure that they are adequately supported by the Word of God. If God has given it, then it will be backed up in the Bible. Whatever sub-points you may use should also be rooted in the Bible. You may also use real life experiences to validate your claim. Be careful, however! Too much life related preaching without any Biblical basis or Christ focus degenerates into a pep rally for the sanctimonious and will not set the captives free. Relate but do not abdicate your position as a herald of God.

Friday

Write rough draft of the sermon.

Regardless of how you choose to deliver the sermon, (Written out in full manuscript, outline, note card or from memory) you must write it out. On this issue I am adamant. This will force you to collect those final little thoughts that are floating around in your stream of consciousness. Write the sermon in full. Since you have already developed your points or principles that you believe that the Lord would have you share with His people on Thursday, pay particularly close attention to the following areas:

Introduction

The first five minutes will tell the difference. You must be able by the power and Spirit of the Lord to gain their attention with a thought provoking, mind-challenging introduction. It does not need to be wordy or lengthy, but it should hit the mark well enough to make them sit up in their seat, nudge their neighbor and say in the words of Dr. A. Louis Patterson, "Let's listen together." If you do not gain them now, it will be harder to pick them up later. Hard, but possible.

Bridges

These are the places of transition between points/ principles/ or parts of the sermon itself. If the bridge is not built properly you force the listener to literally take a leap of faith with you from one point to the next. Remember you know where you are going, but the congregation does not.

Illustrations

Do they have spiritual relevance and significance to the text, thought, theme or thesis, or are you just sharing a good one you picked up at the Ministers Conference or off the radio?

Conclusion

Have you concluded your argument forcefully? Will they grow in the faith because of this word that God has had you plant into their lives? This is what people generally remember more than any other part of the sermon. One preacher says that you start the worship service as a worship leader and you should conclude your sermon as a worship leader.

Topic

Does it match the text? Does it provoke thought, elicit

an immediate "Aha!" or leave the people wondering where on earth "Rev" is going today?

Purpose

Have you remained true to the purpose of preaching this sermon? If it has changed, did you change it or did the Lord change it?

Many preachers debate where to properly start writing the sermon from. Many start at the conclusion because they know where they want to end and write the introduction last. Others just start at the introduction and work their way through the message. Whichever the Lord leads you to do, and it works for you is fine as long as the sermon is Biblically and spiritually correct. My method is to write the body first, point by point. Then write the conclusion, and finish with the introduction. This works for me because of the way I personally gather information, and I am more concerned about the body of the sermon as opposed to shouting the most staid saint off their feet in the conclusion. If the meal is good, not only will you not need desert (you will not have room), but you will forgo the appetizers. (to make sure you have room)

Saturday

Tighten focus, write preaching outline from written sermon.

Time for a final check. Does all your research add up? How do your illustrations sound? Preach through the message a couple of times. How does it sound? Sometimes words that are written well on paper do not sound well to the ear. If you need to make any other adjustments now is the time to do it.

This is the time to put the sermon in its finalized form. If one preaches from a full manuscript, they may want to rewrite it one more time or the exact same size paper they will use on Sunday. Many notebooks can be purchased in different sizes so that if one preaches from this discipline they do not always have to carry a large notebook or folder into the pulpit. **Make sure that you can read your own writing!** If it is done on the computer you can enlarge the text and space it to adjust for your own personal comfort. Make sure that you communicate with words and phrases that are not over the head of the congregation to which you are preaching. It is a crime of ego to preach with a manuscript just to make sure that you include certain references that your seminary dean would give you an "A+" on and will impress your preaching peers but the congregation is left reaching for an encyclopedia, thesaurus, dictionary, and other research books but no Bible.

I develop an outline based on the final written sermon. This not only aids my memory, but it allows me to take just the Bible into the pulpit with a one page (if that) outline. This outline is reduced in size so it can slip easily within whichever Bible I choose to use. In this outline I only write down the points/ principles or any other information that I want to convey to the congregation. I trust God that the Spirit of God will bring all the other information back to my remembrance and my testimony is that He has not failed me yet! However, you can and should not use this method unless you have done the appropriate amount of study.

An outline can be developed from all the information gathered but not necessarily written into a sermon. In this form, you select only those things that you believe the Lord would have you to say and arrange them in some type of chronological order. Then you trust God to not only bring all things back to your remembrance but to make sure that it is put together properly. If your research is not solid and you do not have a masterful command of the English language and a near perfect memory, leave this type of presentation alone.

Finally, one can simply stand up and deliver what the Lord has given them to say. This method requires the highest level of preparation and study to be done effectively. The key is effectively! It is one thing to preach sans manuscript or outline if one has done all the research, study and devotional time that has been described in this book. Those who refuse to do at least that and still want to stand up and proclaim "Thus saith the Lord" are lying to themselves. I am not against preaching without a manuscript for I do it many times myself. I am against preaching without a manuscript and no study of the text or topic. Just running idyllic thoughts or judgmental themes together for the sake of talking. One should never stand up claiming to do the Lord's work unprepared, not knowing where they are going or what they will be saying. Theological and biblical laziness will get you nowhere fast. You will not impress anyone by filibustering over theological imperatives thinking yourself to be wise and showing yourself a fool. Thus, will you fulfill the words of Shakespeare's *"MACBETH"* Full of sound and fury, Signifying nothing. (9)

With the structure firmly in place, we move now towards the day of proclamation and presentation we will make on behalf of the Almighty to His people.

Notes on Section III Chapters 5-6

1. Andrew Murray, *With Christ in the School of Prayer*. Christian Classics Ethereal Library: http://www.ccel.org/m/murray/FirstLesson.htm

2. Harold A. Carter, *Myths that Mire the Ministry*, pg "110 Copyright 1980, Judson Press, Valley Forge, PA

3. Thomas G. Long, *The Witness of Preaching*, pgs. 127 - 129 Copyright 1989 Westminster/John Knox Press, Louisville, KY.

4. Dr. Robert Houston, "*Expository Preaching On-Line Class,*" (www.newhopefriendship.org/class.htm) Used by permission from the E. K. Bailey Conference on Expository Preaching.

5. J. Grant Howard, *Creativity in Preaching*, pg #29, Copyright 1987, Zondervan Publishing House, Grand Rapids, MI

6. Fred B. Craddock, "*Overhearing the Gospel*"

7. Vines-Shaddix, pg#91

8. Wayne McDill, *The 12 Essential Skills for Great Preaching*, pg# 150, Copyright 1994 Broadman and Holman, Nashville, TN.

9. William Shakespeare, *MACBETH* Act 5; Scene 5

Section IV

Presentation

"To whom God would make known what is the riches of the glory of this mystery among the Gentiles; which is Christ in you, the hope of glory:

"Whom we preach, warning every man, and teaching every man in all wisdom; that we may present every man perfect in Christ Jesus:

Whereunto I also labour, striving according which worketh in me mightily."
Colossians 1:27-29

There was a dance show in the early seventies called "Dance Fever." The host of the show would come out and do his little choreographed routine before addressing the audience. Every week there were four couples from around the country vying for the trophy of the best dance team. All of the contestants would be judged in four areas: Rhythm, Choreography, Originality, and Style. The amazing thing was that every time these four individual categories that the contestants would be judged on were spoken, the host saved "style" for last and he always made some type of dramatic gesture of his hands, body or head to accentuate the importance of the individual style of the performers to their overall score.

A similar analogy can be made to the presentation of a sermon. The "choreography" of the sermon would deal with how the sermon is put together and the intricate twists and turns it takes from beginning to end. The "originality" of the sermon would deal with the fresh focus of the text coming from the preacher's personal perspective, not seeking to overtly replicate, duplicate, or plagiarize others material. It is safe to say that both of these categories belong safely in the chapter dealing with the preparation of the sermon.

However, "rhythm" and "style" are issues of presentation. Many of our sermons can adequately pass the homiletic and hermeneutic tests of seminary professors and our pastoral peers. The seminaries and Bible colleges have done a wonderful job in preparing their respective students for this task. Yet on the issue of properly presenting the prepared material many ministers, both experienced and inexperienced would say that we all could do better.

If our presentation is inadequate or ineffective, then our sermon at the very best falls far short of the mark that we aim to hit every Sunday. That "mark" is to be effective in the evangelism of sinners and in the empowering of the saints. It is to challenge people to raise their standard of living to a higher level in God. It is to enlist their support in the work of the ministry. To encourage the saints of God be a willing and working witnesses for Christ in every area and arena of life; to discover the spiritual gifts that the Lord has given them to use for the Glory of God in building up the local congregation.

This is the final bridge to cross. We have bridged the gap between the homiletics and the hermeneutics. Drawing on the theological thought of Gustaf Wingren, Richard A. Jensen helps us to cross the bridge we just have created. He writes "we have not understood the indispensable connection between God's word and human life. We have tended to see these realities as having an independent existence....The task facing the preacher has traditionally been thought of as bringing these two independently existing realities into relationship with each other in the sermon." (1)

Now we must clear the chasm between the herald and the hearers. The way we make that connection is by refining our adeptness at presentation. Inadequate or a bad presentation of a sermon, no matter how well prepared is akin to serving a gourmet meal on a filthy garbage can lid to your friend or fiancée ...... unappealing,.... unappetizing,.... unacceptable.

Dr. J. Alfred Smith, Sr., Senior Pastor of Allen Temple Baptist Church in Oakland, California and Professor of Preaching and Christian Ministries at American Baptist Seminary of the West writes in the forward of Dr. Jeremiah A. Wright, Jr.'s book *"What Makes You So Strong?"* "No matter how well prepared a sermon is, the preacher must be prepared to present the sermon in an exciting, but acceptable manner. A well written dull sermon puts hearers to sleep." (2)

"Exciting..." Let the minister of the Gospel reclaim their fire and fervor and present well prepared messages from above. Let them always remember that it is not a performance but a passion. A Holy calling. One that stands out and stands above every legislated, elected and nominated position in this world. One that has earthly and eternal consequences every time a minister stands before the people of God. If the sermon does not grab you, don't grab it! Leave it in the study for another day.

In their book, *"Preaching the Story* two parish pastors by the names of Ronald J. Allen and Thomas J. Herein write "When my hearers sense that a part of the biblical story has become my story, they are invited to make connections with their own stories." (3)

"... but acceptable." The pulpit is neither the Apollo Theater nor the local night club. The people did not come to see you regardless of what your ego may say. If you think that they have, either you have deluded yourself or you are a thief. Robbing God of the Glory due His Holy name. We are not the Sunday morning entertainment, but we are there to entertain. (to keep, hold, or maintain in the mind; to receive and take into consideration) Manipulation of emotions for personal benefit, histrionics, and other unethical approaches to sermon presentation must be repented of and buried in an unmarked grave.

When you observe the ministry, mission, and message of the Lord you will readily agree that He was a very persuasive presenter of His case. He had an unusual color (originality) and command (style) of the language to those whom He was speaking. When He was finished it always, whether uttered or not called for a commitment on the part of the hearers. That is effective presentation. Effective presentation is to be able to communicate the gospel of Jesus Christ effectively in the language of the hearers to challenge them to commitment.

J. Grant Howard in his book "Creativity in Preaching" declares "Effective preaching.....takes place when the truth of the text works its way into the preacher, roaming through the corridors of his mind and heart, and then like a spring run-off after a winter of deep snow, it bursts over the spillway of his own life and plunges down into the minds and the hearts of the congregation. The thirsty drink. The tired are refreshed.

The dirty bathe. Then, as the rushing waters slow down they begin to form placid pools along the banks of one's life; mirrorlike surfaces that people can continue to gaze into, reflecting their needs." (4)

A word is in order here. We must be careful that we do not throw our sermons over the heads of the hearers and leave them ignorant of what we have said while we are patting ourselves on our backs for using dime a dozen words that are not even in our own vocabulary. In like manner it is also wrong to teach an eleventh grade class from a second grade lesson plan. Jesus was able to communicate at different levels to different people. **He did not fault them for not being at his level.** He simply went to where they were, ministered to them where they were and sought to elevate their conceptual understanding of his ministry and message from there. The Apostle Paul declares

"I am made all things to all men that I might by all means save some." (I Corinthians 9:22)

The better prepared and presented sermons attempt to give as many as would receive, something to take with them when they leave the Group Worship experience. Young and Old, Elders and Junior, Well to do and working class, Literate and illiterate.

I certainly do not want to offend my clergy brothers and sisters, but it is also true that we must be careful not to preach to impress other preachers.

I know that last statement hurts but it is nothing

but unadulterated truth. Even when we are not in the pulpit we will "tune up" in public gatherings away from the church, conferences, conventions or any other time when other ministers may be present and like a competitive bodybuilder "flex" our vocal intonation, pitch and "hoop" as if to say:

"Look at what I got….Can you do this….Will hoop for food….Call me, I can close the show…." With all sincerest apologies to the late Thomas Dorsey, the beautiful expression in faith and trust in the Lord written in "Precious Lord" could almost be rewritten to say…

"Hear my cry…...hear my squall
Hear my drive…...Rise and fall.
Take my card
Pastor please
Give me a call"

Sometimes we are guilty of preaching and presenting sermons simply to gain revivals and major opportunities of preaching, without seeking the Lord's will and word for the occasion. Pastor's Anniversary, Homecoming, City Wide Revivals, Church Anniversary, are all seen as major events in both the life of the church and the preacher who is asked to give the message. It seems that perhaps on either a conscious or a subconscious level, that we realize that no one can exalt you but the Lord but also no one can promote and recommend your preaching like another pastor. If the pastor that has invited us is not pleased with our sermon, then regardless of what his people say, that will be the last time we preach in that pulpit while he is the pastor. He will not recommend you to preach anywhere else either. So, we do occasionally tailor the message for the benefit of the pastor of the Church and not the people of Christ so that we can keep those engagements coming.

Yet have we really considered, or have we just plain forgotten the people in the pews? Those we are called to minister to are often left perplexed shaking and scratching their collective heads wondering what the Lord's Word was for them that night. Some have even walked out of the church wondering what was wrong with them. They did not understand what the preacher was saying but "with all those preachers and pastors up there hollering and having a fit, they couldn't all be wrong so it must be me.....I'm not where I should be in the faith.....What is wrong with me?"

In the area of presentation, we want to deal with the issues of rhythm and style in the delivery of the sermon. An effective delivery opens the physical ears of the hearers to the sermon while it is the Holy Spirit that opens the spiritual ears and hearts of the hearers. There is a Russian proverb that can very well be applied to the preacher. It states

"It is the same with men as with donkeys; whoever would hold them fast must get a very good grip on their ears."

Rhythm

Even Higher Standards Than Yours Baptist Church, a highly educated, silk stocking, hat flaunting, deeply traditional and liturgical church had been vacant for over two years. It seemed as if none of the prospective ministers that the church was primarily interested in and was hotly pursuing were interested in them. And all the ministers that had shown an interest in the pulpit vacancy somehow came up unqualified or undignified in the eyes of the pulpit committee. Since the church constitution stated that the recommendation of the five-member pulpit committee had to be unanimous in order to vote, they had hit a wall. Disagreement was quickly giving way to dissension throughout the church as Sundays came and went with no agreement from the pulpit committee to interview or recommend anyone for the position of pastor.

Finally, the membership of the church convinced the Deacon's that they "needed to have a meeting" to get to the bottom of this. Meeting day came and the pulpit committee was called on the carpet for not presenting someone for the church to vote on. When asked what was wrong with a particular candidate that seemed to be a church favorite, an elder deacon, who had migrated north from Georgia who served on the pulpit committee muttered "No flow, no go." When asked about an associate minister who had applied the deacon said, "No flow, no go." Questioned about a distant family member who had just finished their doctoral dissertation, the deacon shook his head emphatically and said, "No flow, no go."

The church membership was irate and promptly declared that this elder deacon was unfit to serve on the committee. They desired to vote to take him off the committee and replace him with someone else that knew what they were doing. They labeled him as un-learned and ignorant. If they could just get rid of him, then perhaps they could have a new pastor in place be-fore the year ended. That way they could stop being the laughingstock of the community. After all, why wouldn't anyone want to be their pastor - the minister for such a fine church as this?

However, the deacon chair, although younger than this deacon had a great amount of wisdom. He re-quested that the elder deacon explain himself and this curious statement of disapproval of these candidates before things got too far out of hand.

The elder deacon gingerly stood and wiped his sad teary eyes on his dirt streaked tattered neckerchief and said:

"Bruthas and Sistahs. I din't mean no harm or de-lay. I was glad to do y'all this service and I tried to do the best I can. If y'all need me to step down then dat don't bother me none. I don't want no confusion over me. I admit dat I don't know all these big words that these prechas been saying, but I does know what I hear. Every precha I heard talk din't flow. Some talk at you like they some slick talking con artist, all fast like trying to sell us something we don't want. Some talk like de done forgot what da Lord done told em to tell us, like de don't know what de going say next. Some be up there just a reading some piece of paper like it the first time de done seen it or heard it. Some talk so high and mighty dat Eben y'all don't know what he saying either. But y'all just shame to admit it.

I may not know like you know, or can say it like you can, but to me da precha words sound like the music back home in Georgia. When da sun goes down over da red clay hills, and da soft wind blow thru da trees, you hear the music of all da Lord's creatures…..frogs, birds, crickets, hound dogs, chillen playing in the evening light….you feel the pulse touching you, moving you, stirring you, inspiring you. You want to express dat good feeling what is inside of you. Begin to sing or pick at a guitar, blow a harmonica, or play a piano….you just play what you feel on the inside of you. Sometimes fast, sometimes slow, sometime all in da same song but it always touches da soul. Hot jazz, cool rhythm and weepy blues all come from within. Some folks wonder where it come from. It din't come from no man it just flow from da Lord. And I reckon dat both music and da preacha gotta be inspired by God. It just flow from da Lord to da preacha and it flow from da preacha to me. And if it no flow, it no go with me"

That is what rhythm is in preaching. I would define it as the ebb and the flow of a sermon. The movement and progression of ideas throughout the span of the message from introduction through conclusion. It is not set to a musical meter or a poetic meter. It carries the hearers up a mountain, suspended only by our train of thought, pulling themselves along on the handholds and footholds of our words until they arrive at the summit of our thought or point; viewing the vista with excitement and possibilities, only to be led down by the preacher into the valley of discovery of the text to find another mountain to climb.

When combined with an effective rate of delivery (the amount of words spoken in a minute) and a variable pitch in delivery (highness or lowness of sound; avoiding a monotone) the smooth delivery rhythm of a sermon will only aid the minister to better convey to their congregation "What the Spirit has to say to the church." (see Revelation 2:7)

Style

Style is defined as "A mode of expressing thought in language; a manner of expression characteristic of an individual, period, school, or nation; overall excellence, skill, or grace in performance, manner or appearance. (6) The Bible speaks to us concerning an effective and empowering style of presentation:

"Not only was the Teacher wise, but also he imparted knowledge to the people. He pondered and searched out and set in order many proverbs. The Teacher searched to find just the right words, and what he wrote was upright and true." (Ecclesiastes 12:9-10 NIV)

"And it came to pass, when Jesus had ended these sayings, the people were astonished at His doctrine: For He

taught them as one having authority, and not as one of the scribes." (St. Matthew 7:28-29)

Haddon W. Robinson simply defines style as "our choice of words." He goes on to say "Everyone possesses style - be it bland, dull, invigorating, precise - but however we handle or manhandle words becomes our style. Style reflects how we think and how we look at life. Style varies with different speakers, and a speaker will alter his style for different audiences and occasions." (5)

Simply put, one's particular preaching style is not who they were, what they were, or what they do, but rather what they said and how they said it. Unfortunately, too much of the discussion concerning one's preaching style has focused on the particular mannerisms and delivery of a preacher rather than the substance of the sermon.

Show over Style

Truth is that too many ministers are all for giving a good show or a great performance. Everything else takes a backseat. Once diagnosed as primarily a young preacher's disease, it has now infected at many levels in the ranks of clergy and is no longer isolated to any one particular geographical area, race, school, or denomination. Robes are flashier and flashier. Suits are more and more expensive. Handkerchiefs longer and now transformed to color coordinated hand towels with one's names embroidered in a matching color.

You better not even think about wearing shoes from last year this year.

This sense of "showmanship" has even infected our style of delivery. God has blessed many pastors around the country with tremendous ministries and audiences to spread the gospel of Christ. They are unique in who they are. I admire them for what they have done for the Body of Christ and for the Glory of God. I give the Lord all the praise for them. But there are too many cheap imitations that are popping up across this land.

Would you like to get the likes a Manuel Scott, Caesar Clark, Gardner Taylor, Donald Parsons, Jasper Williams, E. K. Bailey, T. D. Jakes, Tony Evans, Eddie Long, Jerry Black, Frankie Ray or whoever else you would personally list here to come to your church and preach for you? Are you afraid they won't come because your budget is tight and you cannot afford to bring them in. If you are scared to even ask them because you have already presumed they will turn you down because you are still in the "Ministry or Church Minor Leagues" and therefore do not have anything to really offer them for coming to you, don't despair! There are always a few bootleg copies around at a discount rate.

Anybody ever purchased a bootleg copy? Ever seen or heard one? These bootleg copies will give you the same sound and perhaps even the same sermon as your first choice. They may even display the same idiosyncrasies that make these gifted ministers unique. They will pop their suspenders like Manuel Scott, holler like A. Louis Patterson, shock your sensibilities like a Donald Parson or a Johnny Ray Youngblood, make you wait for it like Caesar Clark, tell you to "Get Ready" like T. D. Jakes or animate the story like Jerry Black. But they will do it at a rate that will fit into your church's budget this year.

Not to be unfair but female ministers are guilty of the same charge. Too many are bootlegging off Iona Locke, Carolyn Knight, Juanita Bynum, Barbara Amos, Jackie McCullough, Jonnie Coleman and many others.

Remember when Michael Jordan was in his prime in Chicago? Do you remember the commercial that had a chorus of children singing: "Like Mike. I want to be like Mike." Have you not even thought it strange that preachers that have preached to our young folk about "not being like Mike" but be yourself at the same time they were trying to be like C. L. Franklin, Jasper Williams, et al?

It does not always have to be a minister that is on a national stage. Local preachers and pastors suffer the most from the "bootleg" syndrome because they may not be known in certain places. Therefore, a preacher can join a church, learn what he can, move to another location, unpack his bags and reproduce what he has bootlegged from someone else. After all, who is to know, except God? I believe that many preachers imitate both show and style because of two reasons alone:

- We want no less than the same level of success in the ministry as the one we are imitating.
- We do not believe that if remain faithful to being who we are and what we are that God will take us to whatever level it is that we want to go.

Which reason is yours? It does not matter if it is our pastor, the moderator, the pastor of the biggest church in town, state president or tele-evangelist. The motives are often the same. This is not just the ministry desire either, but the money. There are some great qualities in all these ministers. Learn from them. Meditate and think on them. But it is important to remember that there is a difference in assimilation and imitation.

Assimilation is a natural process that naturally occurs when preachers are involved and working together for the work of the kingdom. You will naturally pick up on things, unbeknownst even to yourself. The way you stand, or the way you say certain words. Your body language can all adapt in the assimilative process of working together with other pastors and preachers. **Imitation** is to intentionally try to copy some else, usually without their prior permission. In assimilation you can weed out the negatives; in imitation you do not because they do not concern you; all you desire is the result. Whatever you do, just be yourself.

Discovering the Right Rhythm and Style for You.

When is your delivery too slow, or when is it too fast? Are your mannerisms and expression overly flamboyant or are you as stiff in presenting the gospel as those lethargic members are in praising the Lord that you complained about at your last minister's association meeting? Does it even matter as long as we are telling the "old, old story?"

The answer is a resounding yes. It does matter. As ministers of the Gospel of Jesus Christ we want to be as effective as possible in our presentation. Some of us are more gifted in our exegetical ability to find unusual points in a familiar text than we are in our actual preaching. Some are gifted storytellers and have a provocative imagination but rarely scratch the dust off the text we propose to preach from. Others are excellent writers of sermons, have great analytical minds and have a way with words but their delivery of the same lacks passion with their purpose. Still others can intone, moan, squall, holler, whoop and drive to close a sermon with a fire and fervor that almost literally can flip a sanctuary over and shout any congregation to its feet, but the rest of the sermon leaves one wondering what happened to the rest of the meal.

"Be skilled in speech so that you will succeed. The tongue of a man is his sword and effective speech is stronger than all fighting." (6)

Speech that is too fast or too slow is difficult to

understand and frustrating to listen to. A preacher that talks too fast may be sized up like the candidate was sized up by the elder deacon from Georgia as "a slick talking con man trying to sell us something we don't want." The caricature of a used car sales associate comes to mind. Some people will wonder can you really be trusted. If you talk too slowly, people literally wait for your next word and wonder. Not waiting on what you say but when are you going to say it. Some may even question one's capabilities and function of their mind; questioning if you are delivery challenged. However, if there is an overwhelming preference and practice among us as a people it would have to be that a slow delivery is preferred over a fast delivery.

Henry H. Mitchell in his book entitled *"Black Preaching; The Recovery of a Powerful Art"* has written an entire chapter dealing with Personal Style in Black Preaching. Sub headed under that is an interesting area that deals with the use of a slow delivery. Mitchell writes "Another characteristic of **most** Black preaching is a slow rate of delivery... One difficulty is that the selection of a valid Black sample is complicated by the fact that there are**, here and there**, accomplished Black preachers with a truly rapid-fire delivery. On the whole, however, it seems unquestionable that most successful Black preaching uses a significantly lower than average number of words per minute. Black preachers take their time." (7) (italics mine)

Professor Mitchell has put into words the observation and the experience of many preachers. A slow delivery is considered the norm and in some areas considered more spiritual than a fast delivery. Granted that in some arenas it is the rule and not the exception. The majority of the ministers who preach on the main floor of our state conventions and national Conventions overwhelmingly have a slow or deliberate delivery. Ministers who are high strung and animated are cajoled and criticized by both preachers and people alike to slow down if they want to take that step to the next level of ministry. A rapid-fire delivery is seen as one who is unsure of himself and is in a hurry just to be in a hurry. The cries of the clergy "Take your time!" to the one that is preaching is more often than not seen as a word of subtle chastisement instead of much needed peer encouragement. What causes a dysfunctional delivery and is there anything that can be done to deliver us from that dysfunction?

Underlying Causes of the Delivery Dilemma

Before we tie our fellow ministers (or ourselves) to the stake and crucify them for having sermon speak disorder, let us look at a few of the causes of unusual delivery problems.

Stress - When one is under undue stress, it affects the clarity and conveyance of their speech. The pastor/preacher is under enough stress when they understand that their words have both earthly and eternal purpose. The Deacon's ministry should do everything possible to eliminate the cause of undue stress (and not be the cause of it) in the life of the Pastor. The principle of

Acts 6: 1-4 is clear. The deacons were appointed by the people and authorized by the Pastors (Apostles) so that the Pastors could be free to Pray, Prepare, Proclaim, and Perform the Ministry of the Word.

Geographical Location - Generally speaking many people that were either born or raised in the Northern States talk at what is considered to be a fast pace and for many people in the South the antithesis is true. People that are raised in or live in the city usually talk faster due to the higher pace of living as compared with their rural counterparts, where it seems that nobody is in a hurry to do anything. In addition, wherever you pastor plays a part in your delivery as you will end up culturally adapting to that setting after a period of time.

Cultural Influence - The size and type of family one comes from plays an integral part of not only our speech patterns but our personalities as well. If one comes from a larger family, sometimes in order to be heard at the dinner table for example, one has to say what they have to as quickly as possible before someone else cuts them off. Or a child who is an only child that does not get a lot of attention and becomes an introverted type of personality, when attention finally comes their way and they warm up to it they will keep on talking all night long.

Voice Gender Confusion - If a male has a voice that is constantly being defined and interpreted by others as a female voice (not necessarily on Sunday Morning) he will consequently attempt to force his voice into unnatural lower registers of vocal production, therefore affecting his overall voice quality and speaking ability. He may speak or preach extremely slowly to try to make each word as low (deep) as possible or he may whiz along as fast as he can so he can hurry up and sit down because he does not want to even hear his own voice. A female minister may try to transform her voice from a feminine sound to a more masculine and loud sound, believing that the more she sounds like a man, (often translated as being authoritative) the more people will accept her as a minister.

Thinking faster than you are speaking - This is a common problem that affects many ministers regardless of whether they use a manuscript or not. One's mind races far ahead of their speech. Either because they know where they are going and want the listeners to hurry up and get there so "we can hurry up and rejoice" or the Lord has birthed a revelation right at that moment and they do not want to lose it.

Poor Phrasing - Taking a breath at the wrong place, taking too many breaths or not breathing enough can cause you to have a poor sermon delivery.

Specific Church Concerns - These vary from church to church regardless of their location, although some occur more frequently in a rural location and others are found predominately in an urban location.

- *An inadequate sound system* (or no sound system at all) can cause you to strain your voice and place it in an unnatural pitch just to hear yourself.

- A church that has been "culturally trained" to give no more than fifteen minutes for the sermon and you know you have at least forty five minutes before you even start to close will cause you to try to "cram it all in" lest you be accused of being too longwinded by your members and not thorough enough by other ministers

- A congregation that does not challenge the depth of study of the Pastor in order for them to feel like they have learned something could cause one not only to be lackadaisical in their study habits but in their delivery.

- A church that has elevated the music ministry above the preaching ministry will often shut down immediately after the sermonic "performance" is given, for an intermission to be concluded only when (and if) the pastor/preacher begins to tune up at the conclusion of the message.

- A spirit of failure or frustration in either the preacher or the people will adversely affect both content and context of sermon delivery. Exegesis becomes "Eisegesis as everything becomes viewed from a negative perception. The devil has a pernicious way of showing us the problems of our pastorates, the chaos in our church, the misunderstandings of our ministries and draws our focus off of Christ. Once our focus is off Christ we will begin the downward spiral into the depths of despair. Great relief comes to me in understanding that when the Lord sends his disciples out to preach the gospel, they come back overjoyed at the results. Folks were saved, demons cast out, the work of the Kingdom was advancing. And the Lord's response in effect tells me that He did not send them out to fail. So true with you and I as well, the Lord did not send us out to fail. He charges us to follow Him and be Faithful to Him. If we just abide in that calling we shall never fail.

- *"Greater than Solomon" disease* or trying to be seen by the people as being greater than the former pastor, no matter who they are, how long they served and what they accomplished. Elijah had this problem down by the juniper tree. After hearing the threat of Jezebel and forgetting the power of God (Sometimes we pastors "hear" too much and do not "remember" enough), he makes an illogical request, asking the Lord to take the life of his frustrated child. However, it is the oft passed over reason that Elijah lifts that tells me this issue is a problem that can affect ministry. Elijah declares "It is enough, now oh Lord take my life **for I am no better than my fathers.**" (I Kings 19:4) Unhealthy comparisons to those who have gone before, or even to those that we admire can drive us quickly to a place of discouragement and depression.

What Can I Do?

There is hope, preacher! Don't give up the fight. Listen to S. S. Curry who writes the following in the introduction of his book, *"Foundations of Expression; Studies and Problems for Developing the Voice, Body, and Mind in Reading and Speaking"*: "The usual view is that every defect in the use of the voice is associated with some local constriction, and that for every abnormal habit or action some exercise to restore the specific part can always be found. While this is true, it is but a half-truth. Every abnormal action or condition has its cause in the mind. Hence, technical training *must always be united with* work for the removal of the causes of faults, and for the awakening of the primary actions and conditions. This enables the student to become himself conscious of right modes of expression, develops him without imitation or mechanical rules, and produces no artificial results." (8) (italics mine)

Every voice can be better developed for the task of preaching, if this is what you desire. Just because you preach more sermons does not necessarily mean that your voice will automatically get stronger. If anything, the more you preach, the more any deficiencies that you may have will show. If this is an area that you feel deficient in then perhaps you should give up a convention or two or a couple of new suits or robes and do something about it. Take voice / speech lessons from a professional; someone other than those famous preachers tapes you bought at the last convention. This is not and should not be confused with singing lessons.

Establish for yourself a personal professional development program that addresses any weakness that you may have or any goals that you desire to attain. In this program address whatever areas you personally feel you need more work on. If you must reach outside the walls of the Seminary (either because they did not teach you those things there or to do so in that environment might lower others' estimation of you for not being as gifted as they are) to accomplish these goals then fine. Do not worry about what others say, after all this is your personal program and not theirs. This has nothing to do with what others think or say about you and everything to do with what you think and say about yourself!

7

A Parting Word for the Preacher

"Let us hear the conclusion of the whole matter:"
Ecclesiastes 12:13a

Be yourself! I cannot stress this enough. Do not be an imitator or an imposter; be an innovator. There is no one that can beat you at being you. Regardless of your limitations, deficiencies or fears; regardless of whether real or imagined; the Lord knows all those things and still He wants to use you to proclaim His glorious gospel. Use what He gave you to the best of your ability. Do not make any sudden changes in the pulpit that you have not gained mastery of beforehand. Sometimes it may even be necessary to warn your members before you make any changes in your delivery style. After all they have gotten used to hearing you preach however well (or not so well) you think you preach. Anything other than what they have become accustomed to will raise some eyebrows and some questions.

A True Story

About three years ago, I made a conscious decision to make some changes in my delivery style. In reality all I was trying to do was to implement what I could seem to do anywhere else but the pulpit. I think that every minister has had this experience. There were several reasons for this decision on my part.

I felt like in order to make it to that "next level" in my ministry I had to either make those changes or be satisfied being what one acquaintance bemoaned "major league talent that never got the chance to make it to the majors, forever consigned to the minor leagues." He equated it to being nothing more than a playground legend. John G. Whittier has penned...

"For of all the sad words
Of tongue or pen
The saddest are these:
It might have been." (9)

I had seen the tears and witnessed the frustration of too many pastors who either never had the chance or took the chance to do anything more in ministry but preach, pick up the check and preach again. It was not that they did not have a mind for ministry. Sadly, they were often in situations where all the people wanted from them was a song, sermon, and a shout. In order to keep from birthing ministries that they knew would be aborted or killed due to negligence, they just did what the people expected. There were too many ministries I wanted to develop and nowhere I could see to accomplish them. In order to accomplish them, I would have to move on. To move on, I had to change. That was my dilemma.

I wanted to be respected as a preacher. Not just as a pastor, not as a teacher or student, nor as a minister but as a preacher. Granted this is personal and maybe even a bit prideful but it is an honest assessment of that period of my life. All I ever heard from other preachers and church members was "how great my mind was" "what insight I had to a text" "what the Lord had in store for me" but I rarely heard "Come preach for me or Come do my revival." I have enough understanding to know that most of my evening engagements were due more to the size and ministry of my choir than my preaching. To my ears it was the rekindling of the fires of frustrations of many a yesterday as I outlined in the beginning of this book. "You are good, but…." More sermons that God had given to me have been preached in places I have never been and by preachers who have preached them more than I have preached them simply because they had more opportunities and exposure than I have, and I was kind enough to help them when they called asking for help.

As outlined earlier, I suffered from several forms of delivery dysfunction. One of those dysfunctions is that of talking too fast. Being a Northerner, drilled in rote memorization of facts or information as a child and thinking fast on my feet has caused me to have an incredibly fast rate of speech. It is not only in preaching but in general conversation as well. I am constantly being told to stop thinking and talking so fast. In reviewing videotapes of myself I have noticed a startling fact. The more prepared that I am to preach a sermon, the greater rate of words per minute I use while preaching. Since I am not reading points but recalling points, there is nothing there to slow me down unless I consciously (and sometimes painfully) do it myself.

Finally, I was starting to get a little more exposure as far as the ministry was concerned. Although I was not getting many invitations to preach other than in the local tri-county area, I was developing contacts into acquaintances and acquaintances into friendships. Positions I was blessed to be placed in on the local State and National level had introduced me to many great preachers. I was opening my pulpit up to others even if the same was not being done for me. I felt that eventually I would reap the kindness I had shown to others. When that time came, I wanted to be ready - determined not to take the trip to Flunkerville because of a bad delivery.

So, I changed my delivery style. I did the impossible. I slowed down my speech. Slow considering my normal rate of pace for a sermon. Resisting every urge to revert back to what was comfortable for me, I literally held on to the lectern white knuckled and shaking. Doing everything, I could think of to keep from going back to my regular delivery because I knew where I wanted to go. If having a slow delivery was going to get me where I wanted to be quicker, then I would have a slow delivery this month!

After the services were over, one of my deacons came up to me. Normally he is a very talkative jovial fellow, but on this occasion he was more inquisitive than anything. He wanted to know if I was sick! He was ready to take me to the hospital if necessary. He actually thought I was having some kind of stroke. When I assured him that I was not sick, but had merely tried to "take my time" as I have been so often told and scolded by people and preachers alike, he laughed, looked me right in my eyes and told me "never to scare him like that again as long as he was living and I was the pastor."

I learned a few things that day, and much more since then. The members of my church had **adapted their listening to fit my style of preaching.** As a result, I threw some of them off when I made a sudden deviation from the expected. Although many ministers could and still find fault with my delivery, the message was still going forth. God had blessed the proclamation of His Word with many decisions that could be developed into disciples. That was not happening at many of the churches in my area. God had given me favor. He has allowed us to birth ministries in a rural location that many larger urban churches were not doing.

All because they were hearing what their pastor was saying, they have attempted to implement some things and the Lord has blessed faithful service of both pastor and people.

A Final Word of Praise!

Since that fateful day, I have slowed down a few words per minute. I can hold the rate of speech in check until point or principle one. Actually, what I have done is develop another delivery that I use for certain types of sermons only and only when the Lord says so. But so many other better things have transpired.

God has expanded my horizons and enlarged my coasts. I have stood to preach in places that only a few years ago would have been considered impossible, improbable, and insane. To God be the Glory! I am now ministering at a church in a city that I would have never thought in my lifetime I would preach in, let alone pastor. Our ministry has not been limited by location. Those seeds of kindness that were sown are starting to show signs of harvest. The discovery of other gifts and their development have taken place. This book, decried and mocked as a fantasy better left to other more well known, qualified preachers than me is now in your hands. This vision of God has been provided for by the provision of God's people.

And I remain, passionate as ever about being God's servant, desiring more each day not only to be able to be in his presence but to stay in His presence. Until that day comes, I am charged and commissioned to preach His gospel. Paul says it best in I Corinthians 2:1-5:

"And I, brethren, when I came to you, came not with excellency of speech or of wisdom, declaring unto you

135

the testimonies of God.

For I determined not to know anything among you, save Jesus Christ and Him crucified.

And I was with you in weakness, and in fear, and in much trembling.

And my speech and my preaching was not with enticing words of man's wisdom, but in demonstration of the Spirit and of power:

That your faith should not stand in the wisdom of men, but in the power of God."

Notes on Chapter VII

1. Richard A. Jensen, *Telling the Story, Variety and Imagination in Preaching* pg # 67 Copyright 1980 Augsburg Publishing House, Minneapolis, MN.

2. J. Alfred Smith as written in the forward of *"What Makes You So Strong? Sermons of Joy and Strength"* by Jeremiah A. Wright, Jr. Copyright 1993, Judson, Valley Forge, PA.

3. Ronald J. Allen and Thomas J. Herin, as written in the chapter "Moving from the Story to our Story" from *Preaching the Story* pg # 161 Edmund A Steimle, Morris J. Niedenthal , and Charles L. Rice Copyright 1980 Fortress Press, Philadelphia, PA.

4. J. Grant Howard, *Creativity in Preaching* pg # 12 Copyright 1987 Zondervan, Grand Rapids, MI.

5. Haddon Robinson *Biblical Preaching; The Development and Delivery of Expository Messages* pg # 177 Copyright 1980 Baker, Grand Rapids, MI.

6. Quotation taken from *The Husia*, sacred wisdom of ancient Egypt as translated by Maulana Karenga

7. Henry H. Mitchell, *Black Preaching; The Recovery of a Powerful Art* pg # 96 Copyright 1990 Abingdon, Nashville, TN.

8. S. S. Curry, *Foundations of Expression; Studies and Problems for Developing the Voice, Body, and Mind in Reading and Speaking* Copyright 1929

The Expression Company, Boston, MA.

9. John G. Whittier *Maud Muller*

Selected Bibliography

✦ Braga, James *How to Prepare Bible Messages.* Portland, OR: Multnomah

✦ Bowen, Donald H. *Passing the Torch: Changing Church Leadership in a Changing World.* Callao, VA: Sonrise 1998

✦ Carter, Harold A. *Myths that Mire the Ministry.* Valley Forge, PA: Judson 1980

✦ Copeland, K. Edward *Riding In the Second Chariot.* Kankakee, IL: PrayerCloset 1999

✦ Curry, S. S. *Foundations of Expressions: Studies and Problems for Developing the Voice Body, and Mind in Reading and Speaking.* Boston, MA: The Expression Company 1929

✦ Howard, J. Grant *Creativity in Preaching.* Grand Rapids, MI: Zondervan

✦ Jacobi, Jeffrey *The Vocal Advantage.* Paramus, NJ: Prentice Hall 1996

✦ Jensen, Richard A. *Telling the Story: Variety and Imagination in Preaching*

✦ Minneapolis, MN.; Augsburg Publishing House 1980

✦ Jensen, Richard A. *Thinking in Story: Preaching in a Post - literate Age.* Lima, OH: CSS 1993

✦ Long, Thomas G. *The Witness of Preaching.* Louisville, KY: Westminster/John Knox Press, 1989

✦ Martin, William C. *To Fulfill this Ministry.* Nashville, TN: Abingdon, 1959

✦ McDill, Wayne *The 12 Essential Skills for Great Preaching.* Nashville, TN: Broadman and Holman 1994

✦ Mitchell, Henry H. *Black Preaching: The Recovery of a Powerful Art.* Nashville, TN: Abingdon, 1990

✦ Mitchell, Henry H. *Celebration and Experience in Preaching.* Nashville, TN: Abingdon 1990

✦ Ogbonnaya, A. Okechukwu *In Step With the Master.* Chicago, IL: Urban Ministries 1999

✦ Peterson, Eugene *Reversed Thunder.* San Francisco, CA: Harper and Row 1988

✦ Robinson, Haddon W. *Biblical Preaching: The Development and the Delivery of Expository Messages.* Grand Rapids, MI: Baker 1980

✦ Steimle, Edmund A. *Preaching the Story.* Philadelphia, PA: Fortress Press 1980

✦ Vines, Jerry *A Guide to Effective Sermon Delivery* Chicago, IL: Moody 1986

✦ Vines, Jerry and Shaddix, Jim *Power in the Pulpit: How to Prepare and Deliver Expository Sermons.* Chicago, IL: Moody, 1999

✦ Unger, Merrill F. *Principles of Expository Preaching.* Grand Rapids, MI: Zondervan 1955

✦ Wright, Jeremiah A. Jr. *What Makes You So Strong?* Valley Forge, PA: Judson 1993

Biographical Sketch

D. S. Briggs is the son of the late Mabel Lee Briggs and Sterling E. Glover. He is a native of Plainfield, N.J. and was educated in the public school system of both Plainfield and Scotch Plains, N.J. He is married to Danielle A Rome of New Orleans, Louisiana and they are the proud parents of five daughters.

He served as the pastor of the New Store Baptist Church of Buckingham County, Virginia; the Mount Calvary Baptist Church of Freeman, Virginia; the Mount Zoar Missionary Baptist Church of Durham, North Carolina, Senior Pastor and Organizer of Rehoboth Covenant Bible Fellowship in Raleigh-Durham, North Carolina and the New Dora Missionary Baptist Church, St Louis, Missouri. Pastor Briggs is also the author of the book, *"First Things First; Tithing, Giving, and Stewardship in the Local Church"* © 2003, *We Are The Family of God; Learning Loving, Lifting and Living the Word of God* © 2004, *Daily Memo: A 31 Day Guide* © 2022 *From Abandonment to Acceptance; A Celebration of New Beginnings* © 2023, *and Sermons from a Simple Servant* © 2025 all under the Voice of Rehoboth publishing imprint.

He believes firmly that "failure will never overtake you **if** your desire to succeed is strong enough." Finally, he would have you to know...

If you meet me and forget me....

You have lost notthing…..
If you meet Jesus and forget him…
You have lost EVERYTHING!!!

www.ingramcontent.com/pod-product-compliance
Lightning Source LLC
Chambersburg PA
CBHW050447150626
46551CB00029B/1983